To Corby

thanks for the lesson

views of the inner workings

of my airplane —

I'll be seeing the plane

differently from now on

Best Wishes

Jürgen

Polar Flight

Lake Baikal
MANCHURIA
HOKKEIDO
Lena River
S I B E R I A
CASPIAN SEA
URALS
BLACK SEA
SACHALIN ISLAND
Yakutsk
Moskwa
OKHOTSK SEA
Arctic Circle
KAMCHATKA
TAIMYR
KARA SEA
Novaya Semlya
WHITE SEA
NEW SIBERIAN ISLANDS
BARENTS SEA
BALTIC SEA
FRANZ JOSEF LAND
Tromsø
DeLong I.
SVALBARD
Trondheim
Vesterålen
Lofoten
ARCTIC
Longyearbyen
NORWEGIAN SEA
Bergen
BERING SEA
North Pole
GREENLAND SEA
Shetland I.
Wrangel I.
Jan Mayen I.
Færöes
Bering Strait
OCEAN
ICELAND
GREENLAND
ALEUTIANS
Pt. Barrow
Denmark Strait
Reykjavik
ALASKA
Eureka
Resolute
Baffin Bay
Kulusuk
Davis Strait
Søndrestrømfjord
Great Bear Lake
Spence Bay
Cape Farewell
Julianehåb
PACIFIC
Iqaluit
LABRADOR SEA
Great Slave Lake
Baker Lake
Cape Dorset
ATLANTIC
L. Athabasca
Eskimo Pt.
Hudson Bay
Kuujjuak
Churchill
Newfoundland
OCEAN
James Bay
NORTH
Moosonee
Red Lake
Nova Scotia
International Falls
Fort Frances
Montreal
San Francisco
OCEAN
Minneapolis
New York
AMERICA

Polar Flight

Jürgen Fohlmeister

VANTAGE PRESS
New York

FIRST EDITION

Published by Vantage Press, Inc.
516 West 34th Street, New York, New York 10001

Manufactured in the United States of America
ISBN: 0-533-10104-2

Library of Congress Catalog Card No.: 91-91359

0 9 8 7 6 5 4 3 2 1

Dedicated to the memory of my mother, Gisela, who inspired a love for exploration through her deep respect for courage and the search for knowledge . . .

To my father, Friedrich, who taught me to understand the nature of fear (and therefore to be free of it) through his gentleness, inner strength and character . . .

To my friend Pamela Eyden, whose talent to bring to life beauty, generosity and tolerance gave me 'permission' to write this story . . .

And to all ferry pilots who routinely explore new ocean routes in light aircraft. Their courage is astonishing; adventure is their reward.

List of Illustrations

CONTENTS

PREFACE

As a child I remember standing in my father's country garden on a winter's day, alone, looking out over fields and woods on a gently undulating plain, and feeling all the wonder and beauty— still undifferentiated— of being alive.

Stirring deep within was a dawning sense of anticipation about the great adventure that lay ahead, the exploration of this magnificent natural world in all its diversity. I was fortunate; my parents provided a secure, gentle and optimistic home, buffered from the devastation all around, a consequence of the recent war and the economic upheavals in its train. There, on the land, were only occasional ruins and mangled debris; artifacts as reminders of this form of human insanity.

The alluvial plain of my childhood was built up by the Traun river, which for eons had been carrying down gravel from the mountains. The gravel is now covered by a fertile soil which is divided into fields that spread among stands of wood and forests from which the call of the kuku bird can be heard in summer. Wild strawberries ripen along the forest-edge in spring, and herds of roe-deer drift across meadows and harvested stubble fields in autumn. In the distance to the south and southwest, blue mountains stand on the horizon.

On the plain, hereditary landed farmers live in massive country houses dating to the sixteenth century. These houses are built on foundations of a large, square aspect, enclosing large central courtyards. The roofs slope down low over high, second-story windows, and the stone-floored foyers arch overhead in the form of miniature cathedrals arising from yard-thick exterior walls of stone. Chestnut trees grow in the courtyard, and the farmhouse is surrounded by orchards of apple, walnut and cherry trees. Hazelnut bushes line a small wooden cottage. And in this pastoral setting there lies an expansive airport with little traffic, and with blue and white lamps glowing at night along taxiways and runway. On a summer day I would watch the occasional airplane land and take off from outside the fence of tangled barbed wire, and a longing for the freedom of the blue sky grew ever stronger ...

Years later when I had soloed in a Piper Cub at age sixteen I made plans to fly such an airplane across the Atlantic. But thirty more years would pass before I would fly another model of Piper aircraft along that early planned route in the reverse direction after first crossing over the Arctic Ocean to Europe.

The pressures of a crowded world add impetus to the explorer's inclination for solitude and the natural beauty of remote, wide open spaces. Only the physical difficulties of reaching mountain heights, or the polar regions have spared these domains — to a degree — from the encroachment of the merchant-developer and entrepreneur who have historically followed the explorer into newly discovered realms. Shaped by a severe climate, the unsurpassed beauty of these unpopulated regions remains for the moment intact, if not unthreatened. It was the beauty and the solitude of the arctic combined with a passion for flying that ultimately made the trip related here irresistible.

Over the years I've been seduced by the perfectionism of form and unrestricted flow of acrobatic flying. I've crossed the United States on a number of occasions both in summer and in winter, and once I flew to Yellowknife on the Great Slave Lake in the Northwest Territories of Canada. But I had never before piloted an airplane across an ocean. I hope that the newness of the experience penetrates in the narrative of this trip; for me it was a voyage-of-discovery. It is probable that this was the first solo-flight on the route over the pole from Eureka, N. W. T. to Spitsbergen.

The earlier flight to Yellowknife involved long stretches over unpopulated forest, and made a penetration to even higher latitudes to the northeast seem awesome and intimidating. I was better, but not optimally equipped for the polar flight, and it requires no great intellect to realize that a mishap involving a forced landing on the Arctic Ocean would probably result in disappearance without a trace. The sheer isolation and remoteness of the country demands that the will to make the voyage be strong enough to admit the necessary abandoning of oneself to fate. But life is made for exploration, and risks are an integral part of exploration of any kind.

This book is written from the point of view of a pilot and an explorer. It describes the technical and historical elements that brought the flight into the realm of the possible for me personally. Those experiences of the earlier, true explorers that I found to be essential input into my own planning are therefore included. Among these are their discoveries as to the geographical and physical conditions that I could expect to encounter, and their tragedies. Some of the geophysical content of the book reflects my own special interests. The description of scenery is that of the lasting impressions made upon me during the flight. I have not shied away from presenting all essential technical aspects of such a flight from the pilot's viewpoint. But those portions are written in such a way that the non-pilot should be able to follow them easily with a bit of imagination.

Polar Flight

The writer upon return. Bottom: On Longyearbyen Airport, the writer's aircraft is on the left.

Chapter 1

PREPARATIONS

> "A time will come in later years when the Ocean will unloose the bands of things, when the immeasurable earth will lie open, when seafarers will discover new countries, and Thule will no longer be the extreme point among the lands." — Seneca (4 BC - 65 AD)

It was the arctic ice that drew me. The edges of continental glaciers had been described by some as the most magnificent scenery in the world. I thus began to plan a flight along the west coast of Greenland. And each new plan involved more northerly stretches along that coast. The potential difficulties of flying along such a remote coastline— extensive fog, unknown and unforecast high winds, storms and icing— were ever in my mind, when it occurred to me that it would not be more difficult or much more expensive to fly to the North Pole across the Arctic Ocean. Thus, a new plan was laid; I would fly from Barrow, Alaska, across the pole to Spitsbergen.

This was technically reasonable, but seemed to me somehow unsatisfactory. To reach Point Barrow from Minnesota I would be flying mostly over boreal forest. This was certainly attractive, but I really wanted to see also large tracts of tundra and glacier-covered land. By common standards, Point Barrow lies quite to the north. But in reality it is only in about 71° N latitude, and the distance from there to the pole is some 1100 nautical miles over arctic sea-ice only, no glacier ice. Speculating therefore about various alternative routes, the most obvious one seemed finally also to be the most diverse and beautiful.

If one wishes to fly to the North Pole, the most obvious heading— irrespective of the starting point— is a heading of due north. Starting at Minneapolis, such a heading would touch the western shore of Hudson's Bay, and take me right across the Canadian Arctic islands to Eureka in 80° N latitude, on Ellesmere Island. I had dreamed beautiful dreams about those mysterious arctic islands, and the fact that this route would entail a turn at the pole to fly on to Spitsbergen troubled me not at all.

On a heading of due north I would be flying far beyond the horizon— many horizons— behind which lay a dynamic, frozen ocean. I would be scaling a mountain, first encountering on its lower slopes a band of forest— the northern boreal forest— for a distance of one thousand miles. At the treeline begins a meadowland extending for another thousand miles— the "Barren Grounds," or arctic tundra. Then nothing but crumbling rock and gravel, half-covered with ice-sheets flowing almost horizontally to the edges of basins, sounds and fjords where huge chunks break off, only to be welded into the surface ice, which drifts about at the whim of tides and wind. After that, pack ice for 1300 uninterrupted miles over a frozen sea to the pole and on to Spitsbergen.

Early on I would be crossing a succession of ominous boundaries. The first is the southern limit of the "Sparsely Settled Area," with its survival and rescue equipment requirements. Then, the boundary into the "Standard (Barometric) Pressure Setting Area" for the altimeter; this instrument is set to the mean sea-level atmospheric pressure because of the scarcity of weather reporting stations which otherwise relay the actual local barometric pressure. Coincidentally, all runway and airport surfaces are of compacted gravel beyond this point because of maintenance difficulties due to permafrost, and also because of the paucity of traffic. At about the same location, navigation becomes referenced to True North, in place of the North Magnetic for more southern latitudes; the geomagnetic field lines become so steeply inclined beyond this point, that the directional component is weak and easily disturbed by magnetic storms from the sun, rendering the compass unreliable. Other means of navigation must then be employed. Finally, at 68° North latitude, 100 miles above the Arctic Circle, and well to the north of the northern boundary of Hudson Bay, one encounters the 210 mile wide "Distant Early Warning Identification Zone," the DEW-line, with its string of military airfields. At this point, although there are no further "boundaries" to cross, I will have covered only half the distance to the pole.

The decision to fly to the pole was reached about a year before departure. This seemed a comfortable span of time for preparation. My limited means dictated that I would fly in a small, single-engine aircraft. And this suited me well. Although I hold a multiengine rating, I prefer piloting single-engine planes to light twins; the engine nacelles of twins obliterate too much of the view for my taste.

I finally settled on a Piper Arrow III with a felicitous combination of features: This airplane was eleven years old with factory-installed optional long-range fuel tanks in the wings, and its engine happened to have been in use for a little over 300 hours. The age of the airplane was sufficient to depreciate its value from its original price of over $160,000 to $37,500, and was yet such as to be considered a relatively "young" aircraft. The long-range wing tanks held 72 gallons of usable fuel which translates into a range of about 1200 miles, or nearly eight hours of flying time. This capacity I would augment with a 75 gallon "ferry" tank in the cabin, thereby more than doubling the non-stop flying range to about 2500 miles.

The normal lifetime of an engine is 1800 hours, after which it is replaced or rebuilt on the manufacturer's recommendation. Thus, a 300 hour engine seemed to me to be ideal; it had been used sufficiently to be well run in, and was, for practical purposes, a "new" engine. A reliable engine with low oil-consumption was of the first importance on an expedition such as this.

The second consideration is navigation. In populated areas of the world there is a plethora of radio beacons. But in northern Canada the spacing of beacons is hundreds of miles. The main difficulty with these northern beacons is the warning "Subject to unscheduled outages without NOTAM (an official notice)" that one finds printed on the chart for nearly every one of them. Well, I would just have to do without them if they were unavailable. And so long as I was over land that could be managed.

But I had a larger problem. I would have to be able to find the North Pole in an ocean covered with undifferentiated sea-ice. Once, after explaining my route to an experienced long-distance pilot, saying that after the pole I'd follow the line of 16° East longitude to Spitsbergen, he responded with "16 degrees sounds about right, but first you've got to find it." His point was that I needed some form of long-range navigation.

The simplest and least costly form of this is Loran. While this would be excellent for the Atlantic crossing, there is no Loran radio coverage of the Arctic Ocean at all. With Loran coverage unavailable, the remaining means of navigation become quite costly; the increment in cost is not merely a factor of two or three, but one or two orders of magnitude. The least expensive is called "VLF (Very Low Frequency)/Omega," a receiving set of which is priced beginning at about $50,000. Many Canadian arctic pilots use this form of radio navigation despite the cost.

Even more expensive, at well over $100,000, is INS (Inertial Navigation System). The components of both VLF/Omega and INS are heavy and bulky, suitable for jetliners, but one or the other could be adapted to small aircraft. Another form of navigation is via earth satellite. This is excellent for surface ships, but unsuitable for aircraft because of the relatively long time involved in obtaining a fix; the speed of aircraft is simply too great to obtain an accurate position via satellite.

Because of these costs and problems, I finally settled on the oldest form of determining position accurately, *viz* celestial navigation. When that was finally settled in my mind I felt very pleased. With a sextant one is measuring the heavens directly; the earth becomes a small part of the universe, as in reality it always is. The earth's axis of rotation is always oriented in the same direction on the sky. Thus there is nothing more natural than a sextant and astrocompass when navigating toward the north pole of that axis. At the pole, every heavenly body is at its celestial declination, almost by definition, with the result that navigation in its vicinity becomes quite simple.

The light sent out by a celestial body travels along (null) geodesics of space-time until it encounters the earth's atmosphere where it becomes refracted. The sight-reduction tables for the sextant give corrections for this refraction. But after its long path the starlight must pass through the plexiglass window of the airplane before entering the sextant sight. And there, just before it becomes useful to the navigator, the star or sunbeam undergoes its greatest potential distortion.

Knowing beforehand that the sun would be about 20 degrees above the horizon at the pole, I took great pains to determine the amount of that plexiglass distortion before the trip. When, towards evening, the solar altitude was about 20° in Minneapolis, I made a number of comparisons of sextant readings taken in the open air, and through the plexiglass windows. I was happy to find that the differences were well within my "personal error" of measurement of about four or five minutes of arc for that solar altitude and for the window that I expected to use when it would matter. Thus I had a simple and direct means of navigating in the vicinity of the pole. Farther away, before reaching that "inner circle," and later, after leaving the pole, I would rely mainly on that most basic form of navigation called "dead reckoning." By means of this deliberately ominous sounding contraction of "deductive reckoning," one simply points the airplane in the direction of the destination by reference to the azimuth of the sun, or to a compass, and flies on until the clock shows the estimated time of arrival based on an assumed speed over the ground. For azimuthal reference I used a Canada Astro Compass MKII. For solar altitudes I bought a model A-10A Aircraft Sextant manufactured by Fairchild Camera and Instrument Co. of New York. The sextant has an artificial bubble horizon and a time-averager to compensate for slow oscillations in the airplane's attitude induced by the autopilot. Both instruments are of World War II vintage.

Of importance equal to that of navigation is the management of weather. In the age of satellites we have the good fortune of being able to see the weather over every part of the globe. The decision to depart at a particular time can therefore be based on rational information. But that decision remains a judgement:

There was a time when it was thought that if we only had a sufficiently close spacing of weather reporting stations, we should then be able to make accurate forecasts. However, meteorologists working with the non-linear mathematics involved in atmospheric dynamics are coming to a startling conclusion. Rather than yielding increasingly refined models that approach the goal of a perfect forecast, the results seem to suggest that we'll never be able to make accurate weather forecasts. Weather— technically, atmospheric dynamics— seems to fall into a dynamic category called "chaos," wherein even the smallest perturbation on the level of irreducible "noise" can become amplified in unpredictable ways. This has been called the "butterfly effect" because the random beating of a butterfly's wings can influence the course of the weather hours or days later. The research meteorologist Edward N. Lorenz wrote as follows in the Conclusion of what has become a classic paper[1]: "When our results ... are applied to the atmosphere, ... they indicate that prediction of the sufficiently distant future is impossible by any method, unless the present conditions are known exactly. In view of the inevitable inaccuracy and incompleteness of weather observations, precise very-long-range forecasting would seem to be non-existent." It is this unpredictability that one must convert into a probability in making the judgement to depart on a long flight in remote areas.

Fortunately, however, it is possible to form a picture of the general conditions that one is likely to encounter some hours later. If a long weather front lies across the route it's likely to be present even hours later, although it might have moved some. Or if the air is humid enough, and the sun is shining brightly on the land, the probability for scattered thunderstorms and turbulence in the afternoon is very high. Dealing with such weather then becomes the job of the moment when one actually encounters the conditions. And on long-distance flights one actually shapes one's course in such a way as to take advantage of expected tailwinds around low pressure areas, or cyclones, for example. Thus, even though "weather is how you find it, not how it's forecast," the availability of satellite photos is a real boon to the long-distance pilot.

In addition to these short-term weather phenomena, I found it important to understand the overall climatic picture of the region to be overflown. Thus I expected the weather over the Arctic Ocean to be free of weather fronts and quite stable. In contrast, I knew that the flight along the Norwegian coast, for example, would likely involve intermittent rain showers. The only troubling aspect of the arctic climate was the virtually unpredictable occurrence of fogs. As soon as open water appears among the ice along arctic lands, the sea begins to give off volumes of condensing evaporate. This fog then drifts onto the land, and then again offshore, at the whim of shifting winds. In this way, an airport can become completely "socked in" in minutes, as one is flying towards it in perfectly clear weather. The options then are to circle overhead, waiting in the hope of a change of wind, or to fly to an alternate airport which might be hundreds of miles away, and where one runs the risk of finding similar foggy conditions on arrival.

Of course, it is often possible to obtain updated weather by radio. For this purpose, as well as for position reporting or in case of an emergency, I installed a short-wave radio in addition to the two normal VHF (Very High Frequency) radios carried by the aircraft. The short-wave, or HF, would be used for communications over long distances.

The radio that I installed was capable of transmitting and receiving either amplitude modulated (AM) or single sideband (SSB) signals. By convention, all aircraft communications are carried out on the "upper sideband" of a frequency. And this HF radio enabled me to communicate on any frequency between 1600 and 30,000 kiloHertz.

Because I would be flying over seas with water temperatures of -1° or -2° C I paid particular attention to marine survival. I carried an exposure suit, a covered life raft and an extra, portable Emergency Locator Transmitter (ELT) in addition to several flares. The exposure suit is similar to so-called "dry suits" used by divers in cold water. With this suit one bobs on the water like a cork. An experienced ferry pilot told me that this suit is adequate for survival in cold water for several days, even without a life raft.

But the raft was necessary for search and rescue; even though the suit was of a blaze-orange color, rescue aircraft rarely find a person floating in the water without the raft. Besides, under such emergency conditions the extra comfort afforded by the life raft would be extremely welcome, to say the least. I carried a heavy pack containing a self-inflating bright yellow four-man raft. This capacity may seem excessive, but the information available to me suggested that although a two-man life raft would probably support a single person, it would do so only if the emergency occurred in a swimming pool. With the equipment I had along, I could visualize myself wrapped in an orange cocoon sitting in a bright yellow patch tossed about on a rolling sea and transmitting an emergency signal that could be heard by any aircraft near enough to have a "line-of-sight" to the raft, as well as by several satellites orbiting overhead. Including my two ELTs and my radar transponder in the count, I actually had six independent transmitting radios on board. In all, I carried ten radios capable of receiving some form of radio signal: communication, navigation or radar.

During the year of preparation I wrote letters to the aviation authorities of every country whose airspace I would be entering. In response I always received letters notable for their courtesy. I received approval in every case, except from the Soviet Union, which administers Franz Josef Land, a group of arctic islands I had dearly wished to overfly. I learned too late— after my return, in fact— that approval for that flight would probably also have been granted if I'd taken the proper course of action. That course requires one to create a contact with a Soviet sponsor. When I was finally informed of that, I felt very foolish; the solution then seemed so obvious. Instead of this, I had followed the instructions given in the "International Flight Information Manual" published by the U.S. Government Printing Office, and that course of action was doomed to fail.

Along with letters of approval, the aviation authorities of other nations generally sent packages of local air regulations, charts, and requirements. The requirements were often highly detailed. For example, the necessary survival equipment for Canada specified, among many other things, "an axe of not less than five pounds in weight with a handle of not less than 28 inches in length." Only once, during a telephone conversation with Canadian authorities in Ottawa, did I hear a discouraging note. When asked about approval to fly in the Canadian high arctic, the official responded with "it's your neck." That response was so at variance with the helpfulness and enthusiasm expressed by arctic pilots that I attribute it to the narrow perspective of a man consumed with his next career advance on the tenth floor of a downtown building, surrounded by city, for whom the vitality of adventure and the beauties of remote nature are only a source of fear. That, at any rate, was the image generated by my mind.

Although I felt no fear, I was keenly aware of the magnitude of this undertaking. Perhaps too much so, for during the night before departure I found it impossible to sleep. My mind involuntarily called up visions of vast wilderness of many kinds, becoming ever more remote and isolated, and of the many kinds of difficulties and emergencies that I might encounter. I had taken every precaution and had made every possible preparation. But the success of such a venture depends on many elements of mechanical reliability, weather and judgement, none of which can be specified with 100 percent certainty. Strangely enough, the thought that tormented me most was the vision of my carefully outfitted but overgross weight airplane lifting off home base in this hot July, finding myself unable to climb out of "ground effect," and with insufficient runway ahead, sagging back to the surface to plow a swath through the airport fence, weeds and farmers' fields. That, indeed, would have been the most ignominious ending possible to all these preparations.

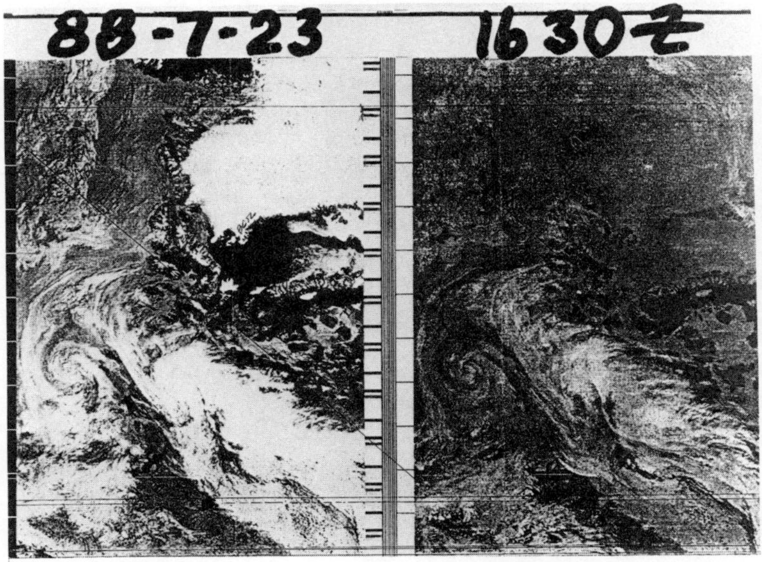

Satellite imagery of the area of the polar route: visual, left; infrared, right.

River delta on the south shore of Baker Lake to the east of the airport.

Chapter 2

TAIGA AND TUNDRA

My father drove me to Flying Cloud Airport. The trunk of the car was filled with travelling gear and it overflowed into the back seat. A few friends and acquaintances met us on the airport tarmac for a warm and heartfelt farewell, although I might have preferred a chance for a quiet final assessment during the departure chores. As it was, I wished simply to get under way as quickly as possible. I transferred the gear from trunk to baggage compartment, the latter already containing an inflatable life raft and an exposure suit for maritime survival. Next came the fueling of the cabin "ferry" tank. I did not need this fuel for the two-hour flight to Fort Frances, where I intended to clear Canadian customs. But this first leg was also a test flight— my first time aloft in an overgross weight condition. The day was hot and therefore provided a reasonably good test of the airplane's overgross flying qualities, even though the ferry tank was only half-filled. I would need a full tank only for the Arctic Ocean crossing. But that later takeoff would occur at a cool temperature and near sea level, conditions under which the airflow over the wing would generate more lift.

The baggage compartment was filled nearly to the top with duffle bags of survival gear and clothing including winter boots, celestial navigation equipment to be used later, a large bag filled with charts, air almanac, sight reduction tables for the sextant and other books, a file of letters and forms of approval from the Federal Aviation Administration and foreign agencies along with the aircraft logbooks, some tools and a rifle as protection against polar bears and for the procurement of food in case of a forced landing on the Canadian arctic islands or on Greenland. I bought two more quarts of engine oil and added them to the six already stored in the baggage compartment.

Up front, in the cockpit, I carried my flight bag, an extra portable Emergency Locator Transmitter (ELT), binoculars, camera, a sandwich, some apples, a mixture of nuts and raisins, a bottle of water, and my communications headset. The Loran receiver was stowed, for the moment, under the right seat.

The flight plan was filed, the walk-around inspection completed, a last minute maintenance bill paid and I was ready to climb on board. But first I took my father aside. I did not want to worry him about the dangers. Indeed, they did not appear large to me. But I wanted him to know that I was not blind to them and that my approach to this trip was reasonably balanced and not simply dominated by a dream. "Many things can happen in a month, whether in Minneapolis or in the Arctic, and if I should not return ..."

It was about midday when I taxied to the far end of the field for takeoff on runway 36. The light winds had conspired to favor the runway that pointed almost directly to the North Pole. I had made thousands of engine "run-ups" before, but this one was accompanied by a strange excitement, as one aircraft departed ahead, and another landed before I was cleared into position for takeoff.

As the airplane lifted off and entered a shallow but steady climb, I breathed easier; after all, the plane was not too heavy to fly, despite the hot weather. In fact, that summer's drought, so hard on Midwest farmers' fields, made the air so dry that visibility extended forever. The complex shoreline of Lake Minnetonka enclosed its blue surface on which sat dozens of sailboats, becalmed. For a short while longer I needed to be careful to avoid the complex manifold of Positive Control Airspace surrounding the nearby international airport, but once across the Mississippi River, which approaches Minneapolis from the northwest, I felt the full freedom of flight. Clusters of lakes lay scattered across my course and the atmosphere had a wonderful, golden glow.

The beauty of long-distance flight is its richness. The land changes. So does the atmosphere and the illumination, sometimes imperceptibly for hours; at others, suddenly. Not tied to the continuous need to follow a one-dimensional highway, the pilot must nevertheless maintain a sense of geographic position and of the airplane's direction of motion. To lose this sense means to be lost. I had the airplane pointed to magnetic north by reference to the gyrocompass or directional gyro (DG), which in turn was set manually according to the reading of the magnetic compass. The initial flight legs of this trip would serve an important function. They would tell me, through experience, the degree to which the DG drifted from its set heading during long periods of straight line flight. A stable DG would be important over the High Arctic, at least on the North American side of the North Pole, because of the failure of the magnetic compass there. This test involved only an occasional comparison of the DG and the compass, and did not detract from the enjoyment of the scenery.

But another navigational chore needed attention; the initializing of the Loran receiver. I engaged the autopilot and, with the operating manual in hand, faced the keyboard of the Loran set, now perched on the passenger side glareshield. In the age of computers, Loran (the word is a contraction of Long Range Navigation) takes on an almost magical quality: At the push of a button the receiver display instantly presents the latitude and longitude of present position to the nearest tenth of a minute of arc, or to within about 600 feet. At the turn of a knob, the display presents distance to, and bearing of any pre-stored "waypoint." Another turn, and the airplane's speed over the ground and the estimated time to the waypoint are displayed. All of this depends on the reception of pulsed radio signals from a "chain" of three or four widely spaced stations whose transmissions cover an area of overlapping lobes extending about 1000 miles from a central point.

My task of the moment was to inform the receiver where it is that I wanted it to take me; in other words, to give it a specific waypoint for navigational reference. I switched to the Waypoint Mode and punched in the latitude and longitude coordinates of Fort Frances airport. Flushed with the success of this (I usually approach computers with marked skepticism), I optimistically added the Red Lake, Ontario, and Churchill, Manitoba airports as further waypoints. After switching back to the Navigation Mode the Loran did its magic and informed me of many things, including my groundspeed of about 125 knots, and that Churchill was 783 nautical miles away.

This fascinating piece of information was in reality "trivia" because it was useless for the moment. And when the time came for it to matter, namely while actually navigating toward Churchill, it would respond, not with distance information, but with "Skywave Warning" and "Station Search" messages. Roughly translated, these messages mean, "hey, how do you expect me to tell you how far it is to Churchill when I haven't the foggiest idea of where we are?" These messages occur when outside of Loran radio coverage and that would be all of that part of Canada that I would cross, as well as the Arctic Ocean.

As a matter of fact, I had the Loran along mainly for the Atlantic crossing on my return, and took the present opportunity to become more familiar with the operation of a relatively new tool of air navigation. But how seductive it is compared to the use of the usual VHF (Very High Frequency) beacons, called VORs, which now seemed incredibly cumbersome. The only problem with greater magic is the greater sense of disorientation and abandonment one feels when it ceases to function.

Mille Lacs Lake was now off to my left. Its blue surface contained slowly changing swaths of sparkle where occasional puffs of wind managed to take hold of the water and stir it to ripple. In the far distance to the right-front lay Duluth, identified by the retreating shorelines of Lake Superior, the whole thinly veiled by a light blue-gray haze. Below was forest land, dark green, but much broken up by brownish yellow-green bogs and marshland with nested patterns of changing vegetation around small ponds. Often the marshland was bisected by deviously meandering streams and small rivers. An occasional road crossed the landscape, here and there flanked by a small farm. And once in a while a small town appeared, confirming that I was not yet over unending wilderness.

Presently, the jagged shoreline of Leech Lake emerged in the far distance to the left, identified by the uninterrupted edge of thick forest. This thick and healthy-looking forest became the background for more and more lakes, which often reflected the wild pines along their shores and on numerous rocky islets, and took on their dark-green colors. On somewhat higher ground a long line of cliffs and bluffs flanked the course of a river for many miles. The imagination paints this line of palisades in a glowing red, a memory from another flight when the setting sun flooded the world with the fire of a dying day. The sky overhead was of a peaceful blue, and yet it seemed as though this color was transmitted through a faintly glowing atmosphere, whose golden hue was most apparent over the horizon. The air was smooth, not a cloud to be seen, and the rays of the sun, streaming through the plexiglass from my left quarter, produced a pleasant level of lighting and temperature in the cabin.

But an airplane in flight always seems to be alive. Even with the engine noise reduced to a low rumble by the headphones, all of the cockpit surfaces seem to bloom with a tingling vibration when one's fingers make contact with them. The needles of the gauges are often minutely blurred by this vibration. The cockpit was of comfortable dimensions for me, but right behind the seatback was a rectangular, stainless steel fuel tank that nearly obliterated the entire cross-section of the fuselage— a heavy monster when full. Bolted to the top of this tank and in the narrow space between it and the top of the cabin, was my short wave (HF) radio. This had its own microphone, held by velcro strips to the front of the fuel tank, and accessible between the two front seat-backs. The HF antenna wire passed through a plastic tube extending downward through a hole in the cabin floor. A small plastic funnel attached to the end of the wire provided drag to hold the antenna horizontally behind the airplane. The length of the antenna was controlled by a reel, which could be set with a friction lock. I intended to use short wave communications on those long legs of flight when I would be far out of range for VHF contact with ground stations. That range was about 60 miles at my altitude.

As I approached Canada I became aware of a distant collection of cumulus clouds all along the horizon ahead. This was the first indication of an active cold front that I knew to be sagging southward somewhere between the border and Hudson Bay, and that would wreck my wish to make it all the way to Churchill on this first day. But from a lifetime of reading travel stories I also knew that such wishful desire has no place on an expedition, other than in planning. In the execution, desire must give way to patience if one is not to increase the risks of the trip needlessly.

As the first widely scattered cloud puffs came to share my airspace I saw a long strip of concrete with clear runway markings, crossed, at about midfield, by a shorter strip, the International Falls airport. Visually scanning the area about ten miles ahead, I spotted the Fort Frances airport, a straight swath cut out of the surrounding forest. I had been descending for some time, and now, from about 2000 feet of altitude I became aware of the gently undulating nature of this forest-covered surface. The depressions were filled with somewhat drawn-out lakes and streams. I circled the airport looking for a windsock. And as I was setting up the approach for a landing to the northwest, caught the Waypoint Alert message dutifully displayed by the Loran receiver. It's nice to see your navigation radio agree with the obvious.

I had already alerted Customs by radio, and a young, uniformed official was casually strolling out as I taxied to the front of the small terminal building. As I stepped down from the airplane, two powerful sensations pressed in on me. Although I had flown barely two hours and no distance at all yet— I was only in 49 degrees north latitude— the immense stillness of the north woods surrounded me, a stillness that was only occasionally penetrated by the twitter of a distant forest bird. The air was pleasant, compared to the sweltering city heat of that July. And in these peaceful surroundings, my body seemed to be trembling and slightly numb. No doubt, this sensation was due to a sleepless night, combined with the stresses of a, for me, momentous departure. Nevertheless, I took these sensations as a warning; flying requires a well-rested body and a balanced state of mind. Days later, at Eureka, I would meet a helicopter pilot who impressed me by following this rule to the letter.

The customs official took one look into this unusually equipped airplane and decided that we'd better get the paperwork out of the way first. I followed him into his office, and after giving name and address I found myself looking into a questioning face; where would I be departing Canada? The answer, Eureka in the Northwest Territories, was to him an incomprehensible departure point. When leaving Canada one crossed into the contiguous United States, or into Alaska, or one might even depart from the Maritime Provinces on a flight to Europe, or Vancouver for the Far East. But there is no logical destination for a departure from Eureka on Ellesmere Island. A few hundred miles from Eureka the World comes to an end— everybody knows that; all you have to do is look at a world map.

I don't think that this official ever really understood my intentions— undoubtedly because of my clumsy description of my plans. But as long as I assured him that I would be leaving Canadian territory, even if it was into a void, he gave me until the end of the month to do so, plenty of time to reconsider my options.

After clearing customs, I called Winnipeg Flight Service for an updated weather briefing. There was no question of making it to Churchill on that day, but I needed to know the precise situation of that nasty cold front; how far could I get? Red Lake, about 160 miles to the north, was probably it, if for no other reason than that there was no other airport for hundreds of miles beyond that point, and the weather front was definitely active. These fronts are the leading edges of huge air masses that seem to be elbowing one another for space. Turbulence and lightning bolts often occur as the new airmass displaces the old, lifting it up powerfully. But, according to the latest satellite pictures, all of the tallest clouds were still comfortably to the north of Red Lake.

I took off and pointed the airplane north. An unending intricately patterned forest and waterscape met my eyes in all directions. I was solidly within the densest part of the boreal forest band, which in this meridian extends as far south as anywhere on Earth. The situation of the continents surrounding the arctic, interspersed by the North Atlantic and North Pacific oceans, causes the various climatic belts to undulate around the lines of latitude. Whether in Eurasia or North America, the southern boundary of taiga (boreal forest) dips farther to the south as one proceeds farther east, away from the warm oceanic influence carried overland by westerly winds.

Flying over boreal forest is an exquisite experience, particularly when headed north. One is surrounded by a vast, pristine expanse with innumerable irregular shapes of water surfaces of all sizes interrupting the unending woodland, which stretches on into the far distance and curves slowly over the horizon, some 80 miles away. The sensation of this natural beauty is gently but firmly crowded by another, uninvited feeling: a sense of abandonment. In lower latitudes, even when flying long distances one takes it for granted that a landing is only minutes away, if the need for one arose. This option is now gone, and primal instincts generate a nonverbal warning of the possible consequences of that loss. This primal feeling is fueled further by the absence of navigation beacons and the scarcity of distinctive surface features.

As I proceeded toward Red Lake, convection clouds became ever more densely clustered, and widely scattered virga and rainshowers broke through the bases of some, making them to appear visually diffuse. The forest and lakescape took on a mottled appearance, dark gray-green beneath the more dense cloud clusters, and shining and dewlike, almost light blue-green over large areas, where in the distance the sunrays penetrated and were scattered by innumerable minute droplets of mist. In the distance ahead and to the left I faced a towering cloud buildup which forced a deviation to the east of course. How many more such deviations would have to be made in the next two thousand miles, before the violent continental summer climate relaxed its grip and relinquished me to the peaceful Arctic? Such detours, simple nuisances in lower latitudes, put to the test one's sense of direction when navigating over wilderness by dead reckoning. Not only do they force one off course, but the massive clouds obliterate the scanty clues to location that one might otherwise glean from the distant surface.

Minutes later, as I was skirting the buildup there was an unexpected cloud-to-ground lightning flash from a benign-looking cumulus structure a short distance off my right wing. Then a second flash from the monster on my left. Fortunately, the sky seemed to clear somewhat again ahead. Just then the Loran receiver announced a Skywave Warning. I pushed the ACKNOWLEDGE button, but a few minutes later the Loran receiver lost its navigation signals entirely; I pushed the power switch to OFF, unplugged the set and stored it under the right seat. The set would not be useful again until I approached Spitsbergen, on the other side of the Arctic Ocean.

I was now tracking the Red Lake VOR inbound. The sky and panorama were still half obscured by convective clouds, but I now saw an occasional dirt road hacked out of the otherwise undisturbed water-landscape on approach to the airport. As the runway came into view it appeared as though it had been stitched together crosswise from two different materials. The glint of the reflecting sun from one half soon made clear that an intense rainshower, with sharply defined edges, had crossed precisely half of the airport, dividing the runway into wet and dry halves with a diagonal line, something I had never seen before.

There is a certain easy feeling as one is approaching the last airport of the day. No longer is the mind burdened with the need to ever update the situation ahead in terms of navigation and the changing condition of the atmosphere and weather. And so it was here. A relaxed feeling came over me. And through this feeling I became aware again of my great love of flying. I only wished that the approach course were a hundred miles long, so that I could fly for another hour or so. But the only thing that remained was the landing check-list: fuel tank, seatbelt and shoulder harness, auxiliary fuel pump on, fuel-air mixture, landing gear down and locked. And as the power was reduced and the airspeed waned, I set the propeller control so as to be ready for immediate take-off power in case a deer were to wander onto the runway. Finally, I added the last notch to extend the flaps fully for landing.

As I stepped down from the wing of the airplane, the peace of early evening had settled on the forest. Towering clouds stood in various directions. But they only stood there with immense billows on all sides radiating pure light of many warm hues, and the pale blue sky reached infinitely deep into the heavens between them. An immense stillness pervaded the land. I found a single person rummaging about in the huge cavern of an open hangar. He was the Chief Pilot of the local flight operation. He helped me to fuel my plane, and gave me the information necessary to obtain a weather briefing early the next morning.

Balmertown and Red Lake are twin hamlets situated well within the otherwise Sparsely Settled Area. They exist by mining— gold mining, among others— and wilderness tourism, mainly fishing and hunting. The hotel in which I stayed was built on bare ground, with only an attempt at a landscaped lawn. It was a somewhat daunting thought to be in about 51° of latitude and already be so isolated with another 40 degrees to the North Pole. But I slept well in the cool air nonetheless.

Next morning I filed a flight plan to Churchill, Manitoba, in 59° N latitude, with the everpresent isolated thunderstorms forecast all along the way. These eternal thunderstorms and rainshowers of the continental summer could not be coerced to part and open a clear way to my destination. I took off in midmorning with scattered convection clouds already building in all quadrants of the sky. But the air was still smooth, with only an occasional bump as I flew into an unseen rising thermal. The airplane was pointing due north.

For the moment the cloud-bases were quite high, at 7000 or 8000 feet, and shining a pure white in their scattered patchwork of domes and filaments and streamers. They cast irregular dark patches on the forest which again spread unendingly before me. I could see individual perfectly formed pines in miniature pointing to the sky. Together, these pines formed a vast carpet of dark green. But the carpet was mottled with a chaotic and intricate pattern of lakeshore lines. Many curving lines also crossed the carpet where meandering streams had cut their beds. The carpet is of a relatively open weave, and the trees do not appear to crowd one another, such as one might expect to see over deciduous forests in other parts of the globe farther south.

The clouds slowly increased in size, and the spaces between them formed small canyons and caverns. The walls of the canyons had very irregular indentations, and streamers of cloud drifted into the open spaces from all directions both above and below. After passing the densest portion of one of these motley lines of cloud, a somewhat more open atmosphere exposed a distant surface of extensive water. The shore outlines were as chaotic as before with many twists and turns into long backwaters and connecting channels and irregular peninsulas and islands. But there is an overall outline to this waterland of Island Lake which provides the pilot with a navigation fix, or anchor point. And sixty miles farther on there is another, called Gods Lake.

The denser cloud areas now seemed to come at intervals, with more open areas of clear air between them. Many of the larger clouds began to cast off virga and rainshowers, framing and transforming the landscape with irridescent glow and diffuse curtains of gray. On several occasions a lightning bolt struck the ground— or a lake— from an isolated darker cloud base. It was weird, and a little unsettling to see these sudden electrical discharges occur without warning while flying in sunshine.

At both Island Lake and Gods Lake the chart marks airports. These are gravel strips, and one of the airport elevations is given only as approximate. Cabins and perhaps houses or lodges mark these as holiday retreats. And an occasional dashed line connecting several lakes on the chart is marked "winter trail."

After Gods Lake, the forest began slowly to thin out. Patches of tundra-like surface begin to appear in 56° of latitude as one approaches the small settlement of Gillam. This town lies on the southern shore of a dammed reservoir on Nelson River, which flows northeast into Hudson Bay. Beyond this point the land becomes soggy as it makes it slow transition— over several hundred miles— to become the Barren Grounds; the tundra.

I had expected navigation from Gillam to Churchill to be quite simple; I'd planned to follow the Churchill railroad line, which passes through Gillam and turns abruptly north some 25 miles northeast of that town onto the nascent tundra. Indeed, I saw the line clearly, including the northward turn to my right-front as Gillam passed abeam to my left. But the atmosphere ahead was dark, and a radio-call to Gillam confirmed the obvious— there was a line of heavy thunderstorms just to the north. By now I was sufficiently remote so that details of this abomination were unknown to ground personnel; I was essentially on my own.

I had seen many kinds of thunderstorms from 5000 feet of altitude. They are all spectacular. They are immense vertical columns of cloud, towering so far above the airplane that it's impossible to judge where they end overhead. And they are broad. Each sits over the land like a fat hippopotamus, and it's difficult to judge the deviation required to circumnavigate the monster. But the bulging domes of some create beautiful structures. With their milky edges sharply defined, they radiate the sunlight in myriads of pastel hues, and fill grooves and indentations with dark shadows, clearly outlined. But the mass of opaque air and extreme turbulence I now faced was not like that.

The thunderstorm ahead was a monstrous heap of a dark greenish gray whose edges were diffuse, and merged only slowly with the somewhat misty air through which I was now flying. The sun had been swallowed by the mist overhead, and the bright and colorful world earlier had now become drab, and there was very little contrast to distinguish features on the surface at any distance. I looked down at the thin line of the railroad track, followed it through its northward turn, and saw it disappear into the dark base of the wet monster. The line appeared fragile and insubstantial compared with the great gray heap of the storm.

I turned some degrees to the right to aim the plane at a point just beyond the diffuse eastern boundary of the storm. As I slowly approached the edge I found myself correcting more and more to the east by small degrees. Soon some overhanging diffuse layers formed a dark cavern, and large raindrops began to shatter on the plexiglass windshield. This was a bit too close, particularly because I now saw several lightning bolts flashing within the cloud. There was a moment of uncertainty; I was flying at the edge of the tundra with essentially no navigational reference, and it seemed to me that this storm was moving eastward— or perhaps southeastward. I could see nothing to the north, and perhaps my one refuge, Gillam, was being overrun by the weather behind. I turned back.

Remaining at a comfortable distance from the stormclouds, I began to circumnavigate this gray haystack-shaped monster around the south. Time seemed to be dragging. But after a while I saw that Gillam, and the reservoir, and the railroad bridge over the Nelson River had not yet been swallowed up.

I continued to circumnavigate the storm, this time to the west where somewhat more contrast was to be seen on the surface; the hope of getting around on this side began to rise a little. And Gillam had informed me that Churchill was clear— imagine, clear; 200 miles to the north was clear and expected to remain so.

But as I neared the southwestern point of the storm with Gillam slightly to the rear on my left, I became aware of a second storm of the same aspect, through the mist just to the northwest of the first. With Gillam remaining my retreat, I continued on doggedly; perhaps I could get through in a space between the two storms. And there, indeed, at the western extreme of the first, I saw a diffuse vertical slit of brightness separating the two dark storms. "Sucker holes," they are sometimes called by pilots, because light ahead in heavy weather can often be a trap that suddenly closes both ahead and behind. But I thought of the clear sky reported over Churchill, and the still open Gillam airport behind, and ventured to continue on in the hope of things clearing before I would reach the point at which good judgement said that I must turn back. Needless to say, I looked back over both my left and right shoulders as often as I looked ahead at the milky white opening.

And the opening was not a trap. Smoothly, but more and more rapidly the brightness widened, and then, even more rapidly, a glassy white undercast unfolded before my eyes. It was of a subdued shade just at first, this layer of milky cloud tops, as it lay there unstirring. But farther on it was quite brilliant. The sky quickly turned blue, and the mountains of cloud began to recede behind, mountains whose green-gray fuzzy edges had cast the world in twilight and threatened to choke only minutes earlier. All tension drained from body and mind. I was over a sea of white cloudtops with no openings at all among them. But the cloudscape was some distance below and its reflections had evidently been responsible for the brightness of the white slit I'd seen earlier. The cloud layer was completely horizontal. Nothing whatsoever towered, or even elevated itself ahead, and I revelled in the thought of a long flight with no obstacles, not even the convective clouds that I'd contended with earlier, and with an outpost on Hudson Bay as my direct destination. The air was wonderfully smooth. And the fact that I had no navigational reference could not depress my feelings of elation.

I settled down to enjoy the slowly passing view of the cloud carpet and sky. Navigation was by a combination of the position of the sun and the magnetic compass and directional gyro which all agreed with one another— more or less. I made an unsuccessful attempt to contact Churchill on 5680 kHz. This resulted in a mental note that I would carefully check the setting of all switches, levers and dials on the rather complicated panel of this short-wave radio while on the ground at Churchill, before continuing on into ever more remote wilderness. After about 45 minutes, breaks began to appear in the undercast. And then, quite rapidly, the cloud cover vanished, and, with it, all brilliance from below. And there lay the tundra spread before me to the very horizon.

But it was a soggy tundra. It was pervasively covered with perfectly round lakes and bogs. The water surfaces of these were of every color, but most of the reds and yellows and greens were of a drab, brownish shade. A few of the lakes were a clear blue, and a few others shimmered of silver as they reflected the sunlight from their rippling surfaces. The soggy land between the lakes was of a brown-green shade of grasses and other tundra plants. The whole presented an extremely mottled appearance, with the lakes and bogs appearing like molds on rotting fruit. And as my gaze wandered to the far horizon, this pattern continued with its elements becoming more and more numerous and more and more miniature because of the distant perspective. The immensity of this lonely landscape engendered waves of joy in my heart; here was still room on this wide planet, room to soar freely; I could well understand the Eskimos' deep love for their land. And the soft blue tinting of the surface colors in the far distance near the horizon confirmed the vastness of this open space.

The Churchill railroad was nowhere to be seen. Instead, I slowly became aware of a white line on the far horizon ahead. That must be Hudson Bay. I estimated its distance as 70 miles, and called Churchill Radio on one of their VHF channels. The white line shone through the bluish horizon more and more brightly, and Churchill confirmed that I was looking at ice. July nineteenth, one day after leaving a dry, blazing-hot midwestern summer with temperatures hovering around 100° F, I was approaching an ice-covered inland sea. The ice had drifted in a few days earlier, the radio operator explained, and then proceded to give me the observations on wind and barometric pressure in preparation for my approach to landing.

From 50 miles out I could see the wide bay that marked the estuary of the Churchill River by tracing its faint shorelines. And then the two mile-long and broad concrete runway appeared as a light gray strip some distance to the east of the river. This runway is the legacy of a former Strategic Air Command (SAC) base, which in years long past shuddered to the rumblings of the noisy B-52s. They are gone now. And the Churchill Rocket Range, prominently displayed on the charts as a huge area covering nearly all of Hudson Bay and large adjacent tracts, may soon follow suit. The range was important as a part of the program of the International Geophysical Year (IGY), for high altitude research, and is now threatened with closure.

I was nearing Hudson Bay. The shoreline on the west approached in a long and low curve that disappeared into the misty horizon to the north. It crossed before me and continued on to the southeast with some low points of land projecting into the sea. A strip of ice lay along the shore in front. And farther out more drift-ice was floating in patches on the deep-blue water. The large bay before the mouth of the Churchill River was to my left-front, and there I could also trace the fine line of the railroad approaching from the south. Churchill inquired as to my preference of runways. Because the light wind was out of the north, and because I had the option of a concrete strip of major airport proportions, I chose it over a shorter, crossing runway of gravel. That seemed to me to be the obvious choice. But the pilot of a larger turboprop transport, who was at that moment about 50 miles to the west, elected gravel. After landing beyond the halfway point of the monster concrete runway, so as to shorten the subsequent taxi distance, I understood the reason. By landing on gravel runway 7, his rollout took him to the front of the terminal building, whereas I still had to taxi the full length of that runway.

I parked the airplane on a concrete platform, next to which was a huge hangar whose size in relation to that of any aircraft now using the airfield is analogous to that of the temple at Karnak in relation to worshippers of human stature. Other airport facilities and offices occupy smaller portions of the same building. The weather office faced to the south, and was entered through a door from a catwalk some 40 feet above the floor along the interior wall of the cavernous hangar. After obtaining a general weather outlook for the following days, one of the airport personnel gave me a ride into the town, which is some miles distant.

Bleached and weatherworn boulders form the exposed backbone of this land along the shore. Fields of flowers grow on larger gravel areas sloping gently to the water. Small stands of weatherbeaten evergreen trees, no more than ten feet high, make their surprising appearance. It amazed me to see trees at all and I expressed this to my companion. I was then informed that those dwarf trees were actually hundreds of years old.

Atop a ridge of boulders sits the weatherworn hull of a twin-engine turboprop transport. It has holes for windows and doors, but is otherwise intact. The airplane had lost power after takeoff and pancaked onto the rocks. No one was injured. But to a pilot driving by it might be a somewhat unsettling sight.

The layout of Churchill consists of a small grid of streets with a long, low and modern Community Center building along the shore. There are four or five small hotels and an Eskimo Museum. The following day I took a boat tour to the star-shaped fortress of massive, but low stone walls sliding and cracking on the solid but plastic permafrost foundations. Insects, especially mosquitoes, were a plague. Then out over the sheet of water formed by the estuary of the Churchill

River, where hundreds of Beluga whales could be observed at close hand. Blocks of ice of every size and shape drifted in lines at certain places near the shore. Rides in a Tundra Buggy were offered in the afternoon, but I needed to go to the airport for a detailed inspection of my HF radio, and to place everything in readiness for my departure for the north on the following day. On my drive to the airport, I saw human figures walking across the tundra, their heads and upper bodies enshrouded like beekeepers in blue-gray sacks of insect netting. A woman rode her bicycle towards an isolated cottage with a rifle slung over her shoulder and a dog trotting after. I assumed that the rifle was a precaution against polar bears, which even at that time of year are occasionally seen in the vicinity of Churchill. I enjoyed a supper with the retired railroad man, Harold Balla, who had brought a tour group out from Winnipeg. Balla is the perfect tour guide; competent and innately cheerful and outgoing.

After breakfast the following morning I filed a flight plan to Baker Lake via Eskimo Point, which lies on the western shore of Hudson Bay at a point where that shoreline begins to turn to the northeast. Scattered rain showers along my route were offered by the meteorologists, and I informed the radio operators to expect a radio call on 5680 kHz to test my HF transceiver. I took off and pointed the airplane towards the western shore of Hudson Bay, which I intended to follow as far as Eskimo Point. I was climbing, gauging the orientation of the curving shoreline, and busy with several other tasks associated with departure, when Churchill decided that it was time for my radio test. I pulled the two plugs of my headset out of the instrument panel, inserted the phone plug into the HF, turned the set on, reeled out the trailing wire and tuned the antenna. The voice of Churchill sounded hollow as though spoken in an echoic cavity. But it was musical and wailing as its tone quality modulated with time, unlike the flat tones heard on VHF. Although I was only a few miles from Churchill, the short wave had the quality of great distance in its timbre. Churchill wanted to try another frequency, 2971 kHz, and I complied; the net result was the welcome knowledge that I still had a functioning HF radio.

To my left stretched the mottled tundra as far as I could see beneath and around the scattered but relatively flat convection clouds. On my right, the blue expanse of Hudson Bay reached out to extensive ice-fields curving over the horizon. Looking out over a sea from 5000 feet it is easy to visualize the world as a globe. Perhaps it is because my mother told me that the world was a ball when I was only three years old, but it would be difficult for me to think that what I was seeing there was a flat earth; the horizon is simply too near for that.

Somewhat closer to shore, several elongated fields of drift-ice interrupted the blue expanse. And almost directly below I saw a single large floe with two captivating features; the white ice contained two rounded splotches of rich and pure color, one aquamarine and the other deep blue. The blue of the sea farther out was metallic in comparison with the pure blue of the splotch. The ice floe looked exactly like a piece of white nougat candy with clear fruit-gel centers. It took me a few seconds to conclude that I was looking at surface melt-pools on the ice. But I had never imagined that these could generate such deep and pure colors when the materials were only clear, transparent water on white ice.

Hudson Bay is very shallow near its western shore and the water below had a muddy greenish appearance. Long and sometimes branching and winding spits of silt meander off-shore. The shoreline itself is sandy, and often the ground appears to be scraped clear of tundra. Some of the exposed rock seemed to be granite, but other low and parallel ridges of gravel are eskers formed by ancient rivers that tunnelled beneath the ice age glacier. Numerous small lakes interrupt the land, and many streams enter the bay by forming irregular small deltas, or by simply widening out to produce submerged sandbars. Eskimo Point lies on such a delta.

As I now turned inland from Eskimo Point I lost the simple means of navigation provided by a coast, and the clouds took on a more obstructing aspect again. Although their bases were at 5,000 or 6,000 feet, and they did not form a continuous overcast, they were all weeping with rain. For an hour or so I flew through this wet air with sunshine breaking through in many places. The tundra grasses and the many irregular lakes had a glassy appearance. There was nothing regular on the surface at all, such as one is so accustomed to in civilization. There, even if one is flying in the desert West, one sees a road or a town now and then. Here, nothing of the kind is to be seen. It is the wild land of the caribou. And because it was summer, it was hard to imagine that these Barren Grounds are treeless because of an intolerable arctic climate. An occasional larger lake in the middle distance provided an updated position fix until I finally acquired the signal from the Baker Lake radio beacon.

The sky was somewhat more clear to the north and northwest and on the horizon I though I could see a long stretch of water that might be Baker Lake itself. It was far away, and its surface was white. But it was a still, peaceful white, not shimmering or dazzling as the ice on Hudson Bay had appeared when I'd first seen it in the distance. It was the first of several puzzling phenomena that would fixate my attention in the Arctic. The white color could certainly be due to ice. But I thought it very unlikely that an inland lake could still be ice-covered in late July, even in 64 degrees of latitude. Every explanation of this puzzling phenomenon seemed to have a fatal flaw. I would have to wait until I was nearer for the correct explanation. Meanwhile, the lakes below were all of an elongated aspect and parallel, oriented about southeast to northwest. These are clearly glacial lakes, and a monster sheet of ice about a mile thick had at one time ground its spreading body radiating outward from the area of Hudson Bay over the rock now covered with tundra plants. In its grinding action the glacier had eroded the grooves that are now filled with fresh water; these lakes are its last legacy.

As I neared Baker Lake the puzzle of the white color was slow to resolution. Not a ripple was to be seen on the white surface; it was perfectly smooth. But several streets of billowing white cumulus clouds hung over the lake. It was these that were reflected in the mirror of the sheet of water. Even so, it was hard to believe that these modest clouds could impart such whiteness to water. But the alternative explanation, that this was ice, was even more difficult to believe, because ice could never be so mirror-smooth.

I have sometimes wondered why the landing runway is so often aligned with my enroute course, so that no maneuvering at all is necessary for the landing approach. Actually, it's not considered good practice to make straight-in approaches at uncontrolled airports. Sometimes, in other places, when I had the straight-in runway in sight far ahead, I've been asked by a radio operator to move to the side to make way for landing airline traffic. But with the rare traffic at arctic airports, I felt that I could take advantage of the efficiency of the "straight-in," and the Baker Lake operator offered no objection. I was floating in a slow descent aimed directly at the gravel strip far ahead at the western extreme of the lake. From a thousand feet I saw a beautifully shaped small river-delta on the southern lakeshore. Some blue spaces of the sky now reflected their color in the ripples near the delta, so that the lake was not ice-covered after all. The blue fingers of the delta-fan are interspersed with broad sandbars that widen out towards the lake. On the northwestern corner of the lake I saw the Inuit village of Baker Lake, fully exposed to this big-sky land on the water's edge of the bush and treeless tundra.

After landing I stepped down from the airplane and saw the colorful rows of boxlike houses of the village from a new perspective, there beyond the airport operations building. The latter is a green sloping structure built on pillars above the ground with Baker Lake printed on it, both in Latin letters and in "syllabics," the highly stylized geometric characters adopted by the Inuit. The terrain is of rolling hills covered with a low carpet of brownish green. An evening peace had settled on the land, and I decided to walk to the village which was about three miles away.

The gravel road was dusty, but the air was perfectly calm. It was wonderfully soothing to walk in my short-sleeved shirt in a temperature of about 68° F. But it was another story to pause for a photograph. No sooner did the swinging motion of walking cease than great numbers of mosquitoes descended on every exposed part of my skin. It was even worse when I decided on a short hike out over the tundra grasses for another perspective to photograph. I must have been fortunate, though, because a mosquito sting is not intolerable, and the horseflies here seemed to be far less aggressive than what I had known in Minnesota. And Black Flies, and other tormentors of a like kidney were happily absent. Their time was earlier in the season, I was told.

Baker Lake is known to connoisseurs in the outside world for its fine Inuit Art Cooperative. The village consists of two rows of small houses along an oil-quenched dirt road, with some more houses extending off in the direction of the ridge about a mile from the lake. A small church with pointed steeple stands near the entrance to the village. Some of the buildings stand on wooden poles driven into the permafrost ground. Beautiful magenta flowers grow in dense clutches along the road, from an otherwise very sparse tundra grass surface. Much of the land in and around town is in fact bare ground. And on this the Inuit youth of the village careen about on small and open four-wheeled all-terrain vehicles. By the time the sun set in the north-northwest in the late evening, all clouds had dissipated and the summer calm was complete.

When I took off the next morning, July 22, white convection clouds hung again over the land. From the vantage point of my low altitude I saw lakes emerging from the valleys of this undulating country. They were blue sheets of water obscured partially by the intervening ridges and points of the green hills. And then I saw it again, a good sized lake with several long indentations into the land of a subdued white surface. Whitehills Lake, it was called on the chart, and I could have sworn that it was ice-covered. But the white color was undoubtedly the reflection of a cloud, although it was difficult to pinpoint the culprit— or culprits— in the sky. Later, after some experience with arctic weather, I found that the wind often falls to a dead calm. The underlying sheets of water then become as smooth as the surface of liquid mercury. These leaden sheets are indeed mirrors of the land and sky. But sometimes the smoothness has the quality of silk, imparting the visual texture of a deep gloss. At those times the reflections of even small clouds become so diffused that their whiteness is uniformly spread over the entire surface. The Norwegian explorer Fridtjof Nansen wrote as follows on September 3, 1893, while traversing some sounds off Taimyr Peninsula on the Siberian coast: "A dead calm on the sea. Fog everywhere over the land. It is wellnigh impossible to distinguish the smooth surface of the water from the ice, and the ice from the snow-covered land. Everything is so strangely still and dead. The sea rises and falls with each twist of the fjord through the silent land of mists. Now we have open water ahead, now more ice, and it is impossible to make sure which it is. Is this Taimyr Strait? Are we getting through? A whole year is at stake! ... No! here we stop — nothing but ice ahead. No! it is only smooth water with the snowy land reflected in it. ..."

The absence of rainshowers on this day gave to the land a more summerlike feeling. In 65 degrees of latitude I crossed a watery area with an extremely complex shoreline, so that the bumpy-edged and convoluted peninsulas themselves contained irregular lakes of many sizes, which in turn contained islands. Then followed a tract of green meadowland. Streams and small muddy rivers crossed the tundra in every direction, flowing in and out of small lakes. The mottled, sunlit surface was interrupted by large, dark patches of irregular shapes where the clouds cast their shadows. But every feature had a pure, pristine quality. The extent of this wilderness is immense, but my view of it was limited by the lower edges of the cloud-banks both right and left.

As the clouds to the left passed behind I saw the broad Back River widening out its muddy brown flow as it neared its estuary on the Arctic Sea. In the far distance to the west, across Back River, the land appeared to be particularly wet with a high density of mostly small lakes. And among these, isolated curved lines of snow or white ice appeared, widely scattered. These white sicles were very few. I saw perhaps four or five at a time out to a distance of perhaps 40 or 50 miles. But they stood out in sharp contrast to the darker wet tundra in that direction. They were remnants of the snow cover from the previous winter, protected against the sun by the occasional fortuitous combination of a crescent-shaped north-facing slope where the snow had accumulated in deep drifts during winter storms.

Back River had reached its easternmost point and turned again towards the northwest as it began its wavy final course to the waters of Chantrey Inlet, when I recognized an unnamed lake from the chart that lay on the Arctic Circle just below. I was then 23-1/2 degrees of latitude from the pole and some 70 miles short of the halfway point between Minneapolis and that initial destination. Fifty miles ahead I saw the blue waters of Chantrey Inlet, which is a long southern bay of the sea channels that parcel out the northern fringes of the North American continent. And as I neared this inlet I became aware of a glaring white line extending along a stretch of the horizon to the north.

Sketchmap of the Canadian Arctic Archipelago.

Chapter 3

THE ARCTIC ARCHIPELAGO

With white ice shining on the horizon ahead, I was about to enter a new domain, a land of arctic islands separated by a labyrinth of sea channels. The islands form a large, roughly triangular archipelago, adding a well-proportioned cap to the North American continent. At the western extreme lies Banks Island; to the north, Ellesmere Island. Completing the corners of the triangle on the southeast is Baffin Land, which forms a kind of loosely fitting lid over the entrance to the inland sea of Hudson Bay. Under the dome of this lid lies Foxe Basin, much of which is ice-covered year round. Indeed, this can be said of all the channels and basins formed by the grouping of the islands. Even after the winter ice melts in August, the straits and channels often become choked with drift ice brought south by winds and currents. The shining ice ahead announced the surface of Rasmussen Basin, which lies on the southern baseline of the triangle that outlines the archipelago.

The labyrinth of channels had for centuries held out the hope of finding a Northwest Passage around the American continent. The latest rediscovery of America by Christopher Columbus during the Age of Discovery resulted in a perplexing problem for those who wished to reach the Orient by sailing west from Europe. Blocking their way was a landmass that seemed to extend unbroken from the Arctic, across the tropics, right down to the Antarctic. Standing atop a mountain in Central America, Nunes Balboa became the first European to spot a sea, the Pacific Ocean, on the other side of the blocking land. Finally, Ferdinand Magellan found a way through to the Pacific Ocean (which he named) at the southern tip of South America. But for political, navigation-technical and pure exploration reasons there remained the wish and the dream of a Northwest Passage around the north of North America.

Over the several centuries the channel-labyrinth was entered, first from the east and later also from the west, but the ships always found their seaway blocked by ice at some point. By the middle of the nineteenth century, John Franklin had found continuous channels through the archipelago, and his successors had traversed them with sleds over the ice. But it was not until the turn of the present century that Roald Amundsen, who would later be the first person to reach the South Pole (some, and I include myself among them, would also add the North Pole [2]), managed to sail through a Northwest Passage with his ship, Gjøa. In the course of that passage, Amundsen left the ship for an expedition to the North Magnetic Pole. This he thought he would find on Boothia Peninsula, which is a northern extension of the land to the east of Rasmussen Basin, that basin whose shining ice-surface I now glimpsed in the distance ahead. The ship, he left in a natural harbor on King William Island on the western side of Rasmussen Basin, at a place named Gjoa Haven, where there is now a fine arctic airport.

I had originally intended to land at Gjoa Haven, but there was a nasty storm to the west, and so held to a slightly more easterly course, directed to the Inuit village of Spence Bay at the southern end of Boothia Peninsula. By my reckoning, this point formed my entrance to the Canadian Arctic Archipelago.

Sparse and intermittent tundra forms the surface of these southernmost islands and peninsulas of the archipelago. But what tundra there still is, rapidly gives way to an arctic desert of gravel and ice as one proceeds to the north. It is a desert not only because of the very sparse plant life, but the annual precipitation is low on the northern reaches of the archipelago. My planned route was nearly a straight line course of more than 1,000 miles from Rasmussen Basin to the northern reaches of Ellesmere Island, right across the center of the archipelago. But what forces of nature formed this group of islands in the first place?

There is no question but that the islands are a part of the North American continental land mass. Unlike Greenland, which is separated from Baffin Land by a deep sea basin which opened when Greenland drifted away from North America under plate-tectonic forces, the islands of the archipelago are continuous with the Precambrian granite of the Canadian Shield, except for shallow channels. My curiosity was aroused: what created the channels that make this northern part of the continent into a beautifully shaped archipelago? I posed this question to the expert of the Canadian Geological Survey after finding no satisfactory answer in other sources.

"Take your pick of theories," was the essence of Dr. R. Thorsteinsson's response. One theory holds that the channels are a complex pattern of "Grabens" (or rift valleys), which are elongated sections of collapsed continental crust, forming broad depressions in the continental surface. Such graben can be found in many places on earth, and sometimes are the first step in the tectonic breakup of a continent; the place for future seas as the continental remnants drift apart. The beginnings of such a breakup may be seen in East Africa, for example.

Another theory holds that the channels were carved by long and actively flowing glaciers during ice-ages. Dr. Thorsteinsson favors this theory. It's well known that fjord coasts were formed in this way, and indeed are still so evolving on Ellesmere Island, for example, where I later observed the mechanism first hand.

My own impression, as a longtime student of maps, is that the archipelago was formed by a combination of the two mechanisms. It seems to me that the northern portion of the continent was at one time under the influence of tectonic stretching forces, and one graben after another appeared as the breaks in the crust occurred and the dominant stress forces shifted to other locations and in other directions, there to eventually cause further breaks. The crustal tension was then eased as one particular break began to open and commence sea-floor spreading about 60 million years ago. At a later time, this spreading halted when sufficient sea-floor crust was laid down to relieve all tension on the northern portion of the North American continent. But the spreading left behind what is now Baffin Bay, Davis Strait and the Labrador Sea between Greenland and the Canadian Archipelago. The theory is then completed by invoking the forces of the ice ages: With the several early grabens in place, the glaciers found in them natural valleys with weakened floors that were easily ground down even further. The subsequent retreat of the ice-sheets, and the accompanying rise in sea level, then filled the valleys with sea water to form channels as we see them today. The topography clearly shows the wear due to flowing ice in many places among the islands. But in other places it also shows faults and narrow valleys indicative of lava intrusions into crustal breaks. These seem to imply ancient tectonic activity.

Irrespective of the theory that formed them, the first waterway along my route to define the boundary between mainland and archipelago now lay ahead, icebound. The clouds around me were slowly thinning, and their tops were lower. It really appeared as though the convective forces were losing their potency because of the reduced surface heating from the low angle of the sun. Or was it perhaps due to the waterways ahead that absorb the sunlight without substantially increasing their surface temperature.

As Chantrey Inlet slowly passed and fell behind on my left, I approached the southeastern shore of Rasmussen Basin. This had a strip of open water along the land, but farther out was covered with ice of a remarkably dark color. The color showed that the ice was decaying as summer advanced. The drab green surface appeared to be scalloped with all edges rounded off, presumably due to the melting action of the sun. The rounded edges were topped with a foam-like froth of subdued white ice. A wide-meshed net of old pressure ridges divided the ice expanse into a quilt patten. It was these pressure ridges and the froth that backscattered the sunlight so brilliantly when viewed from 60 miles away.

I was then approaching Shepherd Bay, which is a DEW-line airstrip about 50 miles to the south of Spence Bay. Shepherd Bay has one of the few radio beacons in these latitudes that was not appended on the chart with the notice, "Subject to unscheduled outages ..." Assuming this meant that the field was staffed, I gave them a radio call. The operator identified himself as "Arctic Radio." His VHF transmissions were crystal clear, suggesting a nearby station; but I have to admit that I do not know with whom I actually communicated. I asked if the ice in the basin was smooth enough and solid enough to be used as an emergency landing field, if necessary. He hesitated to commit himself and wouldn't recommend it.

It was at about this point in the trip that I felt the highest level of uneasiness on this entire expedition. The possibility of some debilitating mechanical problem, or some unforeseen meteorological or navigational difficulty continued to occupy a portion of my mind. By now I felt quite isolated, approaching 70 degrees north latitude with Baker Lake some 400 miles to the south, Resolute some 400 miles to the north, and no intervening landing strip except for the local triad of Gjoa Haven, Spence Bay and Shepherd Bay, here on the DEW-line. Baker Lake seemed to me to be a poor retreat. It was a speck in the middle of the most isolated part of the Barren Grounds with no hangar or mechanical facilities. It was hundreds of miles to the north of Churchill, itself a remote outpost. The thought of limping for hundreds of miles — which meant hours — if even a minor mechanical problem should develop, fueled my uneasiness. But if I lost my bearings because of deteriorating visibility, well, this vast emptiness would rapidly swallow me up. And what about the availability of fuel and oil for my piston engine? I had arranged for it by telephone, but this was the land of the turbine-powered Twin Otter, compared to which my airplane seemed an orphaned cousin. At least one Twin Otter pilot looked ascance at me when I told him that I was not equipped with Omega navigation. The Arctic Ocean was still a thousand miles and several landings away. I looked upon every landing on these gravel strips as potentially full of unforeseen pitfalls. And despite the fact that my isolation continued to increase, that mental burden of concern became less noticeable beyond Spence Bay. Those earlier thoughts were, after all, a response to "what if?" Instead of that I found a captivating landscape, and a calm atmosphere, even if there was a bit of playing tag with an unseen storm to the southwest.

At the northern extreme of Rasmussen Basin there is a peninsula that extends in a southwesterly direction from the mainland on the east. This peninsula, and the land beyond are remarkable on two counts. First, the land surface is virtually black. Second, it has the structural appearance of taffy pulled and drawn-out to the point of tearing. The long, stringy ridges are interspersed by equally string-like bodies of water and long bays. These features clearly were formed by flowing ice.

Boothia itself is a failed island; it would require only a small rise in sea level, or a corresponding fall in the land-bridge of Boothia Isthmus to create an island from what is now the peninsula.

But the land to the northeast on the eastern side of Boothia Peninsula, suggests a complex geophysical history. There the land is transsected with narrow and straight valleys that are oriented in at least three distinct directions. Some of the valleys contain needle-shaped lakes. At one point three valleys form an almost equilateral triangle with sides of about twenty miles in length. These features are strongly suggestive of crustal breaks and lava dykes. Spence Bay lies in the center of this complexity, on the edge of Boothia Isthmus.

I had left the thin cumulus clouds behind, and the sloping gravel-land of Boothia was peacefully bathed in sunshine. It was a uniform light reddish-tan color. I circled the field and landed downhill, to the south, with ice in the bay beyond the strip of open water along the shore. An excitement gripped me, and I was anxious to get out of the airplane and walk this land; it appeared so beautiful, this arctic summer.

The land was an absolute desert. But it was the shape and the peace and the solitude of the country that was so pleasing. A long and low headland reached far out into the bay to the southwest with small islands clustered around and beyond. Some ten miles to the west a height of some 800 feet curved over the horizon. The sun was sparkling on the strip of water between the ice-edge and the land. The colorful, box-like houses of the Inuit village were about a mile to the east, down by the shore where the land was flat, and visible across the barren terrain, which was hilly, sloping upwards to the north.

Two lovely Inuit children accompanied the lineman on his

all-terrain vehicle out from the village. We communicated with signs and gestures and smiles and laughter. But I had to push the airplane up to the fuel-drums. And when the fueling was done the children were nowhere to be seen; I regretted not having snapped their picture. On another trip I will stay awhile in Spence Bay, but my job now was to push north.

When I left Baker Lake, extensive fog had been forecast for Resolute Bay. But when I called them now for a weather update and to file a flight plan, I was surprised to hear that Resolute was clear and expected to remain so for the time being. Such an opportunity was not to be lost, and I took off without further delay.

Climbing slowly to the north, I had a closeup view of the confused terrain of this lower part of Boothia Peninsula. Groups of parallel rows of washboard-like ridges extending in different directions ("dyke swarms") seemed to be elbowing each other for space on the surface below. The packing of such rigid geometric elements is necessarily quite open, thereby allowing much room for a number of good-sized lakes. But the shorelines of these lakes had to contend with the ridge-orientations. These imparted shapes in the form of a T or an L to some of these sheets of water. Some were rectangular with exaggerated corners. Shortly thereafter I crossed several rows of clouds with tops at about 4000 feet.

As I flew on the spaces between the parallel cloud-streets began to fill, and I soon found myself over a solid undercast. I could trace its edges in the distance, both in the east and in the west, where this field of cloud-domes seemed to terminate. It appeared as though these edges followed the coastlines of the peninsula precisely. Evidently the sun still had power over this arctic land to induce thermal convection sufficient to obscure the entire surface with dense clouds. But this power was limited because it could not boost the thermals higher than about 5000 feet. And the air through which I was flying was perfectly smooth.

After 45 minutes of flying on top, the outer edges of the cloud deck began to converge ahead. A large slab of drift ice with thin edges covered the outer portions of Prince Regent Inlet to the northeast. The ice-edge followed the shorelines of Boothia and Somerset Island, but with about two miles of open water along the shores. The surface of the ice seemed porous and rough, as though it were in an imminent state of disintegration. I was still too far south for the permanent thick and durable pack ice. Peel Sound and Franklin Strait to the northwest were free of ice. And beyond them lay the glacier-worn surface of Prince of Wales Island, naked and exposed to the low illumination of the arctic sun.

As the cloud-deck was now breaking up, I saw again a complex topographical surface. Having crossed 71° north latitude, the terrain was dominated by needle-like valleys running north-south and east-west, and also in the two diagonal directions. Needle-shaped lakes and long inlets fill these valleys. Somerset Island and Boothia Peninsula together form a 300 mile long, dumbbell-shaped stretch of land oriented north and south. The central narrows of this dumbbell are not low, being on average about 1000 feet in elevation. But five or six long inlets, each about a mile wide, threaten to slice across the narrows, to create a series of rectangular islands, like a column of bricks. And one of these waterways, Bellot Strait, cuts right across the land in 72 degrees of latitude, and succeeds in isolating Somerset Island to the north. As I crossed the 20-mile long Bellot Strait I was awestruck by the high sides of the valley falling steeply to the dark water below. The reflected banks of the valley imparted this somber shade. And after several more cuts and grooves of a similar aspect, Somerset Island lay spreading before my eyes.

There is something soothing and peaceful in that word, Somerset, and the land did justice to its name on that day. It spread out like a fan into the distances ahead, as the latitudes increased towards the middle seventies, and the sea-channel to the east disappeared over the horizon. I was flying over a desert plateau with some low heights and bluffs rising in a long line parallel to my course in the middle distance on the right. A long bank of clouds lay over the heights. The surface of the land was of a mottled reddish-brown pattern with the upper layer of the heights of a somewhat darker shade. One could almost call it a painted desert. There are one or two large lakes on Somerset, as well as a number of lakelets. But it is the close-meshed net of stream-beds that is more typical of the surface of the island. This is in sharp contrast to the surface of King William Island to the south, which is dominated by lakes of glacial erosion.

This was an easy flight of sightseeing. It was as though I were perched in a high lookout tower that was slowly drifting across this large expanse. It's curious how one's concept of isolation is so relative. The lake country of central Ontario and Manitoba, with its unending expanse of evergreen and birch forests, is considered quite wild and remote when sitting in a living room in Minneapolis. Those are the destinations for fly-in fishing trips to the northern wilderness. By now I was 1500 miles to the north of those destinations — the forest had come to an end long ago, as had the tundra — and yet I no longer felt that heart-clutching sensation of danger that I experienced farther to the south. Was it that I no longer faced towering thunderstorms, or was it simply that I had become indifferent to the danger? No, it could not be that, because I would feel it again in crossing waterways too wide to glide ashore. The reason was that the terrain below offered no obstacles at all to a forced landing, and the country was a land that aspired to the imagination.

A long and pointed bay cuts into the land from the northwest. The northern shore of the bay trends in a north-northwesterly direction until it reaches the sea-channel at the junction of Peel Sound and Barrow Strait. From there it turns north and then to the east in a continuous smooth curve to become the southern shoreline of Barrow Strait. Off the extreme northwestern point lies a small islet with sheer cliffs into the sea. The entire northwestern corner of Somerset Island is a desert table-land, with the table top interrupted by deep, narrow valleys. For a short while I followed the stream-bed of one of these valleys to the shore of the strait ahead.

I had reached the latitude of the northernmost point of Baffin Island. Barrow Strait is a western extension of Lancaster Sound, which is the main entrance into the Canadian Archipelago from Baffin Bay. John Franklin's ships, "Terror" and "Erebus," and, later, Roald Amundsen on "Gjøa," sailed through these sounds before turning south along the western shore of Somerset.

I could easily see the rounded, shield-like height of Cornwallis Island some 35 miles across the strait before me. The entire island seemed to be of a uniform light tan color rising smoothly out of the sea. Rising with the island near its southern shore was a faint strip of a slightly lighter shade, which I took to be the runway at Resolute, nearly aligned with my heading.

I called the Resolute radio operator, gave my position and was informed that the light winds favored the runway ahead, straight-in. He also informed me that the eastern half-width of the runway was dug up and plowed for the time being, but that the other half-width should be adequate for my airplane.

To the west was the large area of open sea called Viscount

Melville Sound. The low sun reflected with a blinding intensity from a large area of waves in that direction. And this reflection increased the misty diffuseness of the western shore of Cornwallis, which trends in a northwesterly direction. I maintained an altitude of 5500 feet to the point over the strait from which I would be able to glide to the shores of Cornwallis with a dead engine. I then began a ten-mile-long final approach, with the small village of Resolute passing off my right just before touchdown on half a runway with an uphill grade.

Resolute is the center of operations in the Canadian High Arctic. Those operations are scientific, that is, geology, paleontology and biology, weather, and military. But the total traffic there is quite miniscule, as one might expect in such remoteness. Resolute lies in 75° north latitude and at the geographic center of the archipelago. In many ways the area around Resolute is similar to that near Spence Bay. All airport surfaces were sloping, and I tried to park the plane so that it would not roll across the field if the parking brakes should fail. Two rows of barracks house the personnel and the excellent weather station. There is also a machine shop, and a cafeteria with limited hours. But as soon as one leaves the area of these buildings, one is out on the desert.

Terry Jesudason, who owns and operates "High Arctic International Explorer Services, Ltd," met me at the airport in a pickup truck. She would not quite admit that she lives in a desert, and pointed out that an occasional Arctic Poppy clings to this crumbling rock. We drove down to a flat expanse lying before the bay, which is ringed by low ridges, and stopped in front of the "International Explorer Home." There a hearty meal was immediately set before me in a truly gentle and beautiful setting. The kitchen and sleeping rooms are slightly elevated, so that the open living room area appears terraced.

This area is of comfortable dimensions, and is filled with leafy plants in stark contrast to the rocky desert on the other side of the window panes. After I had eaten, I was shown to a small room with a comfortable bunk and a small desk. A little later, we had a preview showing of a new videotape on the Arctic Wolf, recently made by David Mech, who was living with the pack that summer on Ellesmere Island.

I was now in a place where one has to force oneself to go to bed— otherwise one would never do it, or so it seems. The sun continues to shine brightly, it only moves to a new position over the horizon. The place was already quiet, but I just had to go out and walk this land. I wandered in the direction of the bay. Slabs of stone and gravel sloped very gently down to the shore, which is about a thousand feet away. The sun stood low over the hill to the north; it was midnight. But the land and the sea lay there, peaceful, illuminated softly by a perpetual golden light. The eastern side of the bay curved widely to the south and ended in a long promontory, or headland, far out to sea. The headland was not high, but it exhibited a pronounced "strand-line" or terrace at its very tip. Along the flanks of the headland I counted eight more terraces, equally spaced between the pronounced one and the present level of the sea, so that the point of land rose out of the sea in steps. The steps indicate past changes in sea level. Arctic lands are rising; they are rebounding from the ice-age when they were buried and depressed by a heavy and extensive ice-cap. Free from their burden of ice, they are reclaiming their domain in the sun. The process appears to be episodic, and the old strand-lines were sculpted by the earlier actions of waves, and of sea-ice grinding against successive portions of the land now above the level of the sea.

I slept well, and after breakfast caught a ride to the weather station with members of a French expedition that was awaiting favorable conditions for a windsurfing trip to the Magnetic Pole, which in this decade lies perhaps one hundred and fifty miles to the northwest of Resolute. The meteorologist seemed to be expecting me because he had already prepared for me a photocopy of a satellite image showing Ellesmere, northern Greenland and much of the Arctic Ocean all the way to Spitsbergen. The Arctic Ocean, on the side toward Siberia, was covered by an extensive overcast, which terminated in a long line from the east of Spitsbergen to just this side of the pole. But the forecast for my longest flight leg of this trip was excellent, with high pressure over Greenland. The only problem was that the storm, which I'd had to the west for several days was now rapidly approaching Resolute. High cirrus streamers ahead of that storm were already pointing overhead. If I waited too long I'd be grounded at Resolute for possibly a week.

I had intended to stay a day or two in Resolute. But a week was too long, particularly because no one could tell what the weather would be over the Arctic Ocean after the passage of the storm. I therefore hurried back to the Explorer Home to pack my bag as quickly as possible. I was sorry to leave that friendly haven in such a rush. But Terry Jesudasen only smiled and said that that was very familiar behavior in her experience. The fickle weather is paramount in the endeavors her establishment serves so well.

The airplane had already been fueled on my arrival the day before. The amount of fuel that I carried this time was carefully calculated so as to allow room for 50 additional gallons after the burn-off during the 350 mile flight to Eureka. This was important because fuel was available at Eureka only by ordering it shipped there beforehand, and only in whole 55 gallon drums. The cost of such a barrel of fuel was about 450 dollars, or approximately four times the price at

Resolute. Actually, I was happy that the price wasn't higher, given the dangerous job of ferrying barrels of gasoline.

This time I took off on the cross runway that pointed downhill toward a low ridge to the southeast. The sea was on my right, with rocky hills to the north and northeast. I turned left to climb over these hills and to cross the 50 miles of Cornwallis Island in the direction of Eureka. The sky ahead was blue and so calm, even though the cirrus harbingers of the storm behind were pointing high across the sky overhead. I continued to climb, and as I did so the whole of Cornwallis came into view with sea channels on all sides. Twenty minutes later I was at the edge of Wellington Channel with Devon Island some 35 miles to the east, and some small islands forming stepping stones to a more substantial peninsula of Devon, which here curves to the west.

The several channels I now faced before reaching the shore of Axel Heiberg Island were all so wide that I would be outside of gliding range to land for about ten miles over each. This caused me some mental struggles because it was possible, by flying a very devious route, or by climbing, to remain within range of land at all times. Actually, from the point of view of the success or failure of this trip it mattered little whether I ditched in the sea or managed to reach land after an engine failure; either way the airplane would probably be destroyed. But somehow it felt more pleasant to think of being on land after such an eventuality. More by default than by anything else I held to my original course with only minor deviations for the purpose of reducing the time spent over water.

The land began to change as I crossed over the western peninsula of Devon Island. Long ridges of folded mountains began to appear on the larger islands. Douro Range on Devon Island is not high. Reaching to about 1500 feet, the ridge is in reality only a series of hills. But its gently curving narrow line suggests the action of tectonic folding. And a few miles to the east of this range, on Colin Archer Peninsula, I saw the first land-ice at an elevation of about 1400 feet.

My course now took me over a large body of water called Norwegian Bay, so named in honor of Otto Sverdrup, captain of the Norwegian ship *Fram,* which was designed and built by Colin Archer to become the first vessel to drift across the Arctic Ocean in the final decade of the 1800's. Sverdrup later discovered and explored the last unknown lands of the Canadian archipelago— those to my immediate north— in the early years of the twentieth century. (Some years later still, the *Fram* carried Amundsen to the coasts of the Antarctic continent on his way to discover the South Pole. . .)

Near the centor of Norwegian Bay are two low islands of oval outlines, one of which is of a considerable size. Some 70 miles to the east beyond water and land I saw a large ice-field, the Sydkap Ice Cap reaching to 5000 feet. It lay there like an extensive and nearly flat white canvas tent propped up in the center by a mountain peak. Low land rose out of the water to the northeast. This land, and the land covered by the Sydkap ice blanket were my first views of Ellesmere Island.

Some 50 miles ahead and to the left the southwestern shore of an island curved toward me out of the north. The mountain terrain farther inland was not particularly high, with peaks ranging from 4500 to 7500 feet. But it was rugged land and covered with glaciers. The curving shoreline to my left-front was abruptly interrupted by a series of deep fjords that cut northward into this Axel Heiberg Island.

As I drew nearer I was awestruck by the majesty of these arctic mountains; this topography was essentially different from anything I'd seen on the islands farther south. I was approaching 78° north latitude, and steep outrunners of long mountain ranges reached in my direction, separated by the several fjords. A thirty-mile-long glacier, deeply crevassed and bounded on its sides by untouched primeval rocky slopes, reached toward me out of the distant height and terminated at the head of the equally long Glacier Fjord. It was wonderful to see so much pristine land, of such beauty, laying there in total solitude, and peacefully illuminated by the eternal sun. Hyperite Point, straight ahead, rose steeply out of the sea with several vertical folds accented by the dark shading of the western sun. The folds reach upward towards an ice-eroded peak.

Ahead stood one mountain range after another, long ridges running about north-south. After crossing Hyperite Point the relief on my left stood so rugged in its beauty and so unending in its expanse and solitude as to be daunting. Deep valleys were filled with dark, smoky-blue shadows, and the mountains farther on were covered by a continuous ice-sheet of all shades of milky blue, as they rose slowly higher to the horizon. This was the Müller Ice Cap.

There are long fjords also to the east, on Ellesmere Island. And in the far distance in that direction was to be seen nothing but ice. But in the near distance the land is a hilly stone desert. And before that, one of the fjords does not terminate, but continues to wind slowly to the north, separating Ellesmere from Axel Heiberg Island.

This Eureka Sound is seven to eight miles wide and was arresting to the eye as I followed its western shore. It curved slowly to the east in the far distance to the north. Its surface was a mirror of the sky. Farther on, large rectangular slabs of milky drift ice lay randomly on the blue surface. The steep flanks of the range along its western shore, steel-blue in the shade and tinted carmine by the sun beyond the bend, were doubled as their inverted image reflected in the still waters of the sound.

A particularly entrancing valley then appeared, extending off to my left. It was broad, and of the characteristic U cross-section betraying its glacial genesis, as did several of the waterfilled channels along my route. This one rose gently from beneath brash-covered water and extended into the mountains where it met the rounded crystal faces of four long-drawn and winding glacier-tongues approaching from various directions. The matte-tan valley floor arose in several rows of tilted rock fences parallel to the trend of the valley. These fences were obviously glacier-worn, and betrayed the unequal resistance to erosion of petrified sedimentary layers that had been tilted on end by tectonic folding. A multitude of snow covered pyramids, some gleaming in the sun, others muted in the smoky-blue shade of soft scattered clouds crowned the horizon far beyond the now receding glacier-tongues.

A short while later as I was approaching the first bend in Eureka Sound, a broad fjord cut eastward into Ellesmere. To the north of its entrance two rounded hill ridges terminate abruptly in steep landslides into the sound. Except for these, and several other short stretches of rocky embankment, only sky-blue and white colors were to be seen in that direction. The land there is quite low. Two broad glacier fields slope gently down to the sea. These terminate along the side of the fjord in calving vertical ice-walls that are reflected in the mirror surface. Scanning slowly to the north of the fjord, the eye meets an undulating hill country covered by fields of snow. Nothing moves. It seems to have been lying there, unchanged, for eons. The strong sensation arose that I was on an unpopulated planet— this could not be the earth. On earth I had always known activity, busyness. And a land of such beauty and peace as this would have been destroyed long ago by their intrusions. And yet the surface below and the sky were earth-like, if somewhat pale in their stillness. It was summer; the wide, blue, unstirring sheet of water spoke of that. Besides, I'd been walking in shirtsleeves a few hours before. Was I dreaming? Sailing above an alien and exquisitely beautiful planet? After my return I was asked several times how it was possible for me to fly over such a wild and forlorn country. In truth, it was the most natural thing for me to do.

Because of the half-loop of Eureka Sound to the east, I was then crossing over the easternmost peninsula of Axel Heiberg Island. Even though its shoreline formed a smooth half circle, the mountains a few hundred feet below were extremely rugged. They were of bare rock, and formed several rows of ridgelines that pointed to the sky with aspects like ax-blades. V-shaped valleys between the ridges harbored streams that flowed over the gravel of small outwash plains on the shores of the sound. The dark shadows, and the golden-red hues of the illuminated crests of the extreme relief below presented a picture of deep contrast, and one of the most beautiful landscapes I'd ever seen.

I was then about 60 miles from Eureka. I had planned to fly outbound using the NDB at Resolute, and then to track the Eureka beacon inbound from about the halfway point. Several times I had switched the ADF receiver to the Eureka frequency, only to find a lazily spinning needle on the Direction Finder's dial. I had also made several unsuccessful attempts to contact Eureka by radio. Well, it did not much matter; my navigation was essentially visual, anyway. The rugged mountains of Axel Heiberg Island were now receding on my left quarter, and I was approaching lower, but still hilly desert terrain. Eureka Sound had completed its wide, half-circle excursion toward the east, and began to trend to the north again. The snow and ice-cover was left behind, and I was looking at a reddish tan land surface bathed in low, western sunshine. On the blue mirror surface of the sound lay several massive ice-blocks.

A rocky desert hill blocked my view of the fingerling Slidre Fjord on whose northern bank lies Eureka in 80 degrees of latitude. As I crossed this ridge, the fjord and a strip beyond it that I took to be the runway came into view. Now, too, I was able to contact the station on VHF, with the information that I was seven miles to the south. I was slowly descending toward a landscape of unlikely contrasts, like something that Salvador Dali might have painted. An untouched, hilly, desert land of a uniform warm, tan color of muted visual texture lay there, completely still, with large areas of abstractly curving boundaries cast in the dark shadows of nearby hills. On a single speck of this expanse stood structures of miniature, but precise geometric outlines. Two tiny spiderlike machines— helicopters— stood before one of these structures down by the shore. Slicing into this land was a smoothly polished surface of the purest blue. On this surface, to my right, lay two large blocks of pure white ice, with many hard edges and emerald green flanks arising from beneath the water. And on my right quarter a single straight line of mountains pushed up above the plain in that direction at a distance of some 30 miles. The mountains were a long series of overlapping rounded domes covered by snowfields with aspects like triangular sails filled by strong winds while on a tack.

I landed to the west, and was met by two young men who directed me to a spot well off the runway to park the airplane. One of the two was the “commanding officer” (for lack of a better title) of this small and diverse community. Because I had never before been met by the mayor of a community upon landing, I began to realize that I represented an intrusion into the work of the people here. I was nevertheless welcomed in the best form of Canadian hospitality. And I take this opportunity to express my appreciation to this CO.

Near the airplane stood long rows of stacked drums of fuel painted yellow and orange, hundreds of barrels lying on their sides and packed to form structures reminiscent of a honeycomb. We rolled one of these barrels up to the airplane and set it upright. But I had second thoughts about fueling the airplane just at once. Perhaps I was overly cautious, but I preferred to let the barrel stand a day or so, so that any particles of dirt could settle out of the fuel before it was pumped into the airplane's tanks. We therefore boarded the crew-van and drove toward the Eureka compound.

The first building I saw was a long, low affair with a short tower of a Moorish aspect, white in color and seemingly made of crepe paper. I am assuming that this crumpled surface was of a material to provide insulation against the intense cold of the arctic winter. I was told that this building was at one time the barrack for a contingency of soldiers. Beyond this building, and down a short slope was another long, low structure. This was the main operations building of Eureka and it housed several small offices, the radio room and meteorological station, the kitchen and dining areas as well as a general recreation room with several pool tables. I noticed that the excellent cook of Eureka set out several varieties of cake and cookies, freshly baked and always available. And on the terrace outside, which overlooks Slidre Fjord, fearless and even aggressive birds of a beautiful design, with pointed wings and long whip-like tail feathers, Jaegers, were ever ready to snap up in flight chunks of broken meat and gristle or potatoes thrown up to them.

Besides these two buildings, Eureka includes several other structures with sheet-metal walls and large doors that serve as hangars for the two helicopters, and mechanical shops. Two rather primitive wooden buildings without toilet or running water serve as barracks for Canadian government visitors. In one of these I spent two nights—that is to say, two periods during which the sun drifted across the northern sky— quite comfortably.

The next day, besides obtaining an updated weather outlook from Resolute Bay, also fueling the airplane with a manual pump, which took an hour's time, and generally preparing myself for the crossing of the Arctic Ocean, I took walks across the sloping gravel landscape. To the northeast rose the tall, charcoal gray Blacktop Ridge. At places, water was gurgling out of the dry ground, soaking it for a short distance downhill. This was groundwater in the form of permafrost whose upper stratum was now melting in late July.

Somewhere in the vicinity there was also a pack of Arctic Wolves. David Mech, who was studying them that summer, kept the whereabouts of their den a secret; understandably so. Paleobiologists had found in the area pieces of wood from trunks of trees that grew a million years before. Evidently this region had known warmer climates in the remote past, and forests once stood where there is now only desert. It is wonderful that remnants of these forests can survive a million years in something like wooden form. This land is very fragile, and even tire tracks will remain imprinted on it for a hundred years. I can only hope that we are sane enough not to destroy it with development of mineral and oil exploration.

As the sun circles the sky, the line of the mountains of wind-filled sail-snowfields to the east-southeast, named

Sawtooth Range by the people of Eureka, continues to change its shade and color. It lies there like a sleeping sentry, a uniformly low ridge of rounded peaks with indentations and valleys angling between, far out on the reddish plain beyond the head of the deep-blue Slidre Fjord. Before the mountain range, and on the fjord surface lay the two massive icebergs. They drifted in on the tide and became grounded there when the tide turned. Now, looking obliquely across from the 100 feet high embankment of Eureka, they alternately reflect their emerald sides in the mirror of the fjord, or stand there on a rippling surface of the purest blue water one could wish to find.

Glacial valley on Axel Heiberg Land. Four glacier-tongues may be seen approaching the head of the valley from various directions.

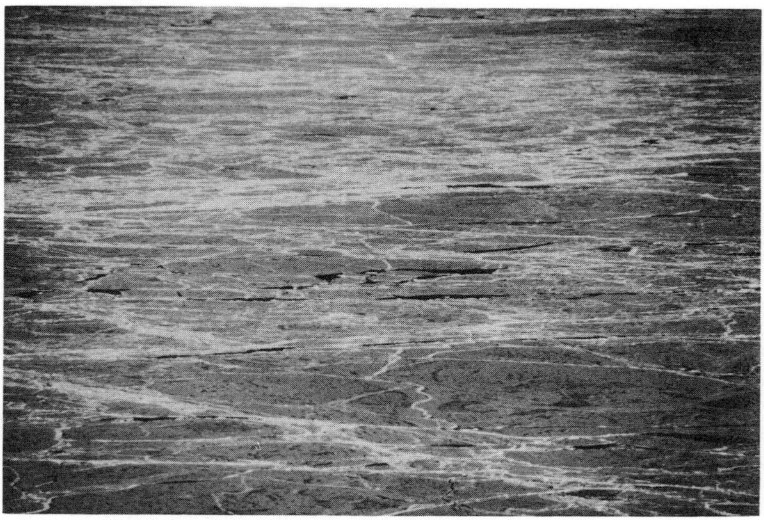

The Arctic Ocean in 89° N latitude from an altitude of about 50 feet. Bottom: North Pole from 5000 feet of altitude.

Chapter 4

THE ARCTIC OCEAN

> "As soon as one has traversed the greater part of the wild sea, one comes upon such a huge quantity of ice that nowhere in the whole world has the like been known. Some of the ice is so flat that it looks as if it were frozen on the sea itself . . . This ice is of a wonderful nature. It lies at times quite still, as one would expect, with openings or large fjords in it; but sometimes its movement is so strong and rapid as to equal that of a ship running before the wind, and it drifts against the wind as often as with it."
>
> —*Kongespeilet* (Norwegian, "The Mirror of Kings," circa 1100 AD)

Eureka, Northwest Territories, July 25, the sun in the eastern sky: Within a matter of hours I would be looking down on the top of the world— circling the point of the earth at which its axis of rotation pierces its surface. That is a singular point of the earth's standard coordinate system, where all meridians come together and terminate.

At the geographic North Pole all hours of the day coexist. One cannot say that it is one o'clock or ten o'clock because at that point all time zones meet. For half of the year the sun circles the sky and shows no daily periodicity in its elevation above the horizon. Thus, there is nothing to distinguish noon from, say, midnight. For three months the sun steadily climbs, circling the sky until its angle above the horizon (the sun's declination in celestial coordinates) reaches

23 degrees, 26.6 minutes. It then commences a slow, circling descent until it crosses the horizon for six months of darkness— the polar night. Except for a single instant during each 24 hour period, the moment that the sun is directly over the Greenwich (zero degree) meridian, two calendar days coexist at the North Pole. Daily variations in the sun's angle with the horizon begin, and slowly become larger as one moves away from the pole towards the edges of the Arctic Ocean, an ocean densely covered for thousands of miles by plates of ice.

This ocean is dynamic. The entire ice surface moves jerkily and with many devious zig-zags across the full oceanic expanse, but with a net movement parallel to a curve that crosses the pole from a point off the northeastern coast of Siberia, near Bering Strait, to a point off the Greenland coast. Surface ice, first frozen north of Bering Strait, takes four or five years to journey across the ocean until it melts in the Greenland Sea, which divides the Arctic and North Atlantic Oceans. Winds, ocean currents and tides drive the ice mass non-uniformly, causing it to crack, opening long "leads" or "lanes," or jamming the ice-edges together. Pressure ridges form as the ice floes clash, their edges bending, splintering, breaking, or sliding one on top of the other. The effect is similar to mountain building *(orogeny)* caused by the jamming together of rocky plates of the earth's outer layer, the lithosphere.

To a degree, the behavior of the ice is a miniature scale model of the tectonic movement of the earth's lithosphere, greatly sped up in time. The ice floes, which have lateral dimensions typically measured in hundreds of feet to several miles, are typically six to 10 feet thick and create pressure ridges typically 10 to 20 feet high. Often one floe is pushed beneath another and the two freeze together, thereby making the ice-crust 20 or even 30 feet thick. After a period of jamming the pressure may be relieved and the floe edges drift apart to form a lead. All of this happens on a time scale of hours. Contrast this to the time scale of tens and hundreds of millions of years for the same phenomena of rock-plate tectonics, according to which continents move about the earth's surface.

The net drift of the arctic ice was discovered accidentally by an ill-fated American expedition. The Jeannette Expedition, under Captain George Washington DeLong, was based on the hypothesis that a branch of the warm "black tide" — the Japanese Kurosiwo Current — flowed north through Bering Strait. This warm water was expected to keep free from ice a large portion of the Arctic Ocean to the north of the strait, much as the warm Northeast Atlantic Current keeps open the sea to the north of Norway. The Jeannette Expedition sailed through Bering Strait in 1879 and was making for Wrangel Island off the northeastern Siberian coast. They thought of Wrangel Land as a cape of a landmass which might reach across the pole as an extension of Greenland. They intended to make their landfall and then sled overland to the North Pole. Given the arctic knowledge and mythology of the time, such a journey seems like a fabulous dream to me. Even years after the Jeannette expedition the belief in a polar land was still held. In an article in *The Forum* (August, 1891), General Adolphus Washington Greely, the American explorer, wrote, "We know almost as well as if we had seen it that there is in the unknown regions an extensive land which is the birthplace of the flat-topped icebergs or the paleocrystic ice."

DeLong and the crew found, however, that the imagined polar land mass does not exist, at least not anywhere to the immediate north of Wrangel Land or the New Siberian Islands. There was also no sign of either a warm current, or an ice-free lobe of the Arctic Ocean. Instead, their ship became set fast by the forming surface ice and began slowly to drift to the northwest with the icepack. A year and nine months later, after difficult struggles with the ice to maintain the physical integrity of the Jeannette, the jamming ice crushed the ship and sent it to the bottom. DeLong and a majority of the crew perished tragically, first by the sinking of a lifeboat during a gale in an attempt to reach the Lena River delta on the Siberian coast, and then of starvation at the head of the delta. Although, judging from his journal (e.g. [3]), DeLong considered this expedition to be a failure, it did discover several tiny islands (now called De Long Islands) in a sea of densely packed ice remarkably far to the northeast of the New Siberian Islands.

Two years after the sinking a number of articles, unmistakably from the Jeannette, were discovered by Inuit (Eskimos) on the southwest coast of Greenland near Julianehåb. The author of the article reporting the find [4] speculated that they could have arrived on Greenland only by drifting on the ice across the pole. Thus was planted the seed for what seems to me to have been one of the most remarkable of polar expeditions: that of the drift of the Norwegian ship Fram from 1893 to 1896 under the direction of Fridtjof Nansen. That trip is chronicled in Nansen's *Farthest North* [5], published in 1897, and is a legendary travel story of discovery.

Nansen had also assumed an ice-free lobe of the Arctic Ocean, in which he intended to sail to high latitudes, his estimate was 78 degrees N latitude. This lobe was thought to be created by the warm waters of the Lena River debauching into a shallow sea. Nansen indeed found his open water spread over a broad continental shelf area to the west of the New Siberian Islands; farther on however, he found the sea to be unexpectedly deep, and to have the character of an oceanic abyss.

Early in that expedition, and despite having already found a depth of over 2000 fathoms (12,000 feet) in the Arctic Ocean, Nansen was still speculating on the possibility of a polar land. On March 9, 1894, Nansen wrote in his journal, "There has been a good deal of ice-pressure in different directions today. Oddly enough, a meridian altitude of the sun gave 79° 45'. We have therefore drifted only 8' southward during the four days since March 4th. This slow drift is remarkable in spite of the high winds. If there should be land to the north? I begin more and more to speculate on this possibility. Land to the north would explain at once our not progressing northward, and the slowness of our southward drift. But it may also possibly arise from the fact of the ice being so closely packed together, and frozen so thick and massive. It seems strange to me that there is so much northwest wind, and hardly any from the northeast, though the latter is what the rotation of the earth would lead one to expect. As a matter of fact, the wind merely shifts between northwest and southeast, instead of between southwest and northeast, as it ought to do. Unless there is land I am at a loss to find a satisfactory explanation, at all events, of this northwest direction. Does Franz Josef Land jut out eastward or northward, or does a continuous line of islands extend from Franz Josef Land in one or other of those directions? It is by no means impossible. Directly the Austrians [Payer and Weyprecht from the ship "Tegetthoff," the discoverers of Franz Josef Land some 20 years earlier] got far enough to the north they met with prevailing winds from the northeast, while we get northwesterly winds. Does the central point of these masses of land lie to the north, midway between our meridian and theirs? I can hardly believe that these remarkably cold winds from the north are engendered by merely passing over an ice-covered sea. If, indeed, there is land, and we get hold of it, then all our troubles would be over. But no one can tell what the future may bring forth, and it is better, perhaps, not to know.

"Saturday, March 10th. The line shows a drift northward [this "line" was a rope to which a bag-net was attached, and hanging about 100 fathoms below the surface]; now, too, in the afternoon, a slight southerly breeze has sprung up. As usual, it has done me good to put my despondency on paper and get rid of it. Today I am in good spirits again, and can indulge in happy dreams of a large and high land in the north with mountains and valleys, where we can sit under the mountain wall, roast ourselves in the sun, and see the spring come. And over its inland ice we can make our way to the very Pole."

The following spring Nansen and one of the crew, Hjalmar Johansen, left the Fram in middrift on an attempt to reach the North Pole by dogsled. They reached 86° 14' N latitude, breaking the old record by about 3° of latitude. At that point they were compelled to turn in order to reach latitudes where they might find game to replenish their dwindling supplies. They spent 15 months roaming the vast polar icefield and the islands of Franz Josef Land where they passed the winter, above 80° north latitude.

The discovery of Franz Josef Land is described by Julius Payer [6] in the following terms; I offer it because it represents one of the rare discoveries in a recent era of new lands in the Arctic Ocean (my translation from the German):

"The 30th of August 1873 (79° 43' latitude, 59° 33' longitude) was a memorable day; it brought a surprise, such as is found only in the rebirth to new life. It was around noon, as we were leaning over the railing, gazing into the driving fogs through which the sun's rays broke now and then, when a passing wall of mist suddenly revealed lines of rough cliffs far to the northwest, which in a few minutes developed into the scene of a radiant alpine land! In the first moment we all stood there spellbound and in complete disbelief; then, carried away by the persistent reality of our good luck, we broke out into the wild cries of joy: "land, land, finally land!" No one was on the ship's sick-list any longer; the news of the discovery spread in an instant; everyone had rushed on deck to secure with his own eyes the certainty that we had before us an uncontestable result of the expedition. Though not through our own efforts, but only because of the lucky chance of our ice-floe and as if in a dream did we win it; but in any case the possibility appeared to be given us to get to know through our own efforts the size and lay of this land, which arose from the ice-desert as if by magic. At the same time our eyes fell doubly painful on our unstoppable drifting floe, on our dependence on its arbitrariness, on the absence of a winter harbor from which alone the exploration of the land could with safety have been undertaken. For the moment however, walking on this land lay outside the domain of every possibility; anyone who might have left our carrying floe would have been cut off and lost; it was only under the impression of the first excitement that we rushed over our ice-field, even though we knew that innumerable cracks made the land unapproachable to us! Having arrived at the edge of our floe, some four miles from the ship, and on fifteen miles distant from the nearest coast, we looked from an ice-height at the composition, mountains and glaciers of this enigmatic land. Back then we thought its valleys decorated with pastures and populated with reindeer, which wiled in the undisturbed enjoyment of their freestate, far from all enemies."

From Nansen's and Payer's, and indeed from the several Russian, English and American accounts it's clear that surface travel over the ice-pack by dogsled (or snowmobile) is possible only in fall, winter and spring. Actually, surface travel is practical only in the fall and spring— September, October, and February through May— because of the continuous darkness during the winter months. In winter, the often spectacular and colorful writhing serpents, and curtains, and light shafts of the aurora borealis are inadequate to illuminate the way. On the other hand by June the upper surface of the ice becomes slush (Payer calls it a snowswamp), up to three feet deep, making surface travel virtually impossible. And later, in July, after the slushy snow has melted on the floes, the open lanes become the major obstacle. But this situation presents no hindrance to an airplane in flight.

As a pilot, I was naturally more concerned with the atmosphere above the polar icefield, the air through which I would be flying. But here, quite happily, I felt no real concern. It's true that in the stories written by arctic travelers I had often read of violent storms. It's also true that books on arctic aviation weather warn of "whiteouts," where clouds, fog and surface ice conspire to scatter and rescatter sunlight so effectively as to make the flow of light completely isotropic, casting no shadows and eliminating depth perception. But these are situations that I felt I could easily avoid by relying on satellite weather images, and waiting for the right day. Furthermore, they are rare occurrences in July and August.

Of greater moment was the common occurrence of widespread fog and low stratus. Arctic climatologists [7] describe as unique to the Arctic the occurrence of stubborn cloud layers extending for hundreds of kilometers. The moisture for these clouds arises from the ocean itself, evaporation from the open leads, and to a lesser extent from surface melt and direct sublimation of the ice. The persistent nature of the cloud decks speaks of the general calmness and stability of the arctic atmosphere. There is no thermal convection due to solar heating of the surface because the surface temperature remains at precisely the freezing level, the temperature of ice water, throughout the short summer. The air over the Arctic Ocean systematically descends from higher strata which are fed by uplifted air along the polar front located farther south. All of this suggests excellent flying weather over the Arctic Ocean.

Despite this, I had two concerns. I had always hoped that when the time came to fly over the Arctic Ocean, luck would smile upon the endeavor and give me unlimited visibility of its surface; it would be a real pain to navigate to the pole only to be looking down on an undercast. And even if it were an overcast instead, it would be somewhat of a disappointment to view a drably shaded polar surface in place of a sunlit icefield, maximizing all of the discriminations of structure and shade, and even color, to be seen there. Besides, a persistent overcast would make solar navigation impossible.

My second concern was with possible icing of the airframe and propeller. I had heard stories of aircraft "icing up" during attempts to descend through polar clouds, although my best information was that this occurs only somewhat earlier, In June, or later in the season at the end of August. One knowledgeable pilot, an Air Force meteorologist, suggested flatly: "Stay out of the clouds." But however good-intentioned, this can't always be arranged on a flight of over 1500 miles with no landing field anywhere along the way.

Icing occurs only if the cloud temperature is below freezing. Two lines of thought led me to expect the atmospheric temperature above the Arctic Ocean to be on the plus side of zero degrees Centigrade: The first was the fact that the upper surface of the ice melts in July, forming large freshwater pools on the ice-floes [5,6]. Whether this results from direct absorption of sunlight by the ice, or because of heat transfer to the ice from a warmer atmosphere, I was not sure; probably a combination of both. In any case, I did not think that direct solar absorption alone could be effective enough to melt the surface in the face of constantly descending cold air; I had lived long enough in Minnesota to know that bright sunshine had no effect on solid ice when it was overlaid by a cold airmass. I therefore expected the descending air over the Arctic Ocean to be relatively warm.

Secondly, in Fridtjof Nansen's description of his drift with the Fram across the polar ice pack, he relates stories of his companions playing cards, on deck, with only sweaters over their shirts at that time of year. The temperature was above freezing, and that warm air had to originate in higher strata because surface-air would necessarily be at the freezing level after being in contact with ice water for a long time, sun or no sun.

If I had reason to expect the air at a few thousand feet of altitude to be above freezing, still, it wouldn't be much above 0° C, and the margin for error was uncomfortably small. There was really nothing to be done but to go out there and see for myself. What I actually found was a remarkably constant temperature of between 3 and 4 degrees C (about 38° or 39° F) at about 5000 feet all the way from Eureka to Spitsbergen. That temperature was completely indifferent to bright sunshine or overcast. Only when I descended to about 50 feet above the surface in 89° north latitude did the temperature drop to precisely 0° C. Just what I expected—the temperature of ice water.

About nine hours before that time I was making final preparations for the crossing of the Arctic Ocean. I packed my duffel bag and lugged it, along with the flight bag, camera and binoculars, up the rocky slope to the mess area in the operations building. After the usual substantial Eureka breakfast, the first order of business was to get a weather briefing; this would decide "go" or "no go." I called the weather office at Resolute Bay by radiotelephone and heard substantially good news: the length of Greenland was still under high pressure, and the latest satellite pictures showed substantially clear air to the north of Greenland and over the Canadian high arctic islands. I imagined that the normal clockwise atmospheric flow around "highs" in the northern hemisphere would give me a slight tailwind component as I flew to the pole and on to Spitsbergen. But, as a matter of fact, my route was so far removed from the northern coast of Greenland that there would practically be no wind at all—maybe three knots of tailwind component. In any case, the decision was "go". I then filed an ICAO (International Civil Aviation Organization) flight plan: Eureka-direct-90° north (North Pole)-direct Longyearbyen, Svalbard. After Resolute Bay read back all of the details, I insisted that they forward a copy of the flight plan to Soviet aviation authorities. If I were to encounter any problems with navigation, there was at least an even chance that my first landfall would be somewhere on the Siberian arctic coast. I did not want such an event to be a complete surprise to the local military.

Resolute was helpful in every way. They told me of two Soviet drifting ice-stations and gave me their last known latitude and longitude coordinates, and a couple of radio frequencies they might be listening on, just in case. One of them was relatively near my route, but the other was hundreds of miles on the other side of the pole. They also reminded me of Alert as a possible emergency field.

Alert is an outpost on the northeastern cape of Ellesmere Island. It lies in 82-1/2° north latitude and was over 200 miles to the east of my route. All of my information said, or implied, that Alert is strictly off limits to civilian aircraft, except in case of distress. From what I could gather, I assumed that Alert is a phased-array-radar station, and I had some, admittedly very dim, hopes that they might be willing to give me a radar fix while I was over the Arctic Ocean. Later, when the time came for me to ask, via HF, they told me flatly that "we have no radar." They were, however, quite willing to courteously relay a position report to Resolute Bay. In fact, my HF contact with Alert was caused by my repeated and unanswered calls to Resolute from 86° north latitude. Alert simply answered and offered to help. Shortly after that I lost all radio contact for hours.

After filing the flight plan, the "CO" sat down with me to settle my bill. It came to the equivalent of 440 U.S. dollars for two nights' lodging in a barrack and meals, plus the compulsory use of their crew-van to and from my airplane. This exorbitant amount is actually understandable, when one considers the cost of maintenance, and shipping materials and groceries to this remote outpost. I have rather fond memories of this "CO," and indeed of all the personnel stationed at Eureka. A couple of them were young "apprentices" in meteorology, always in high spirits, and seemed to be living out a fantasy by "camping" for a time at an outpost in the high arctic. The "CO" took excellent care of me, considering that I was an uninvited guest in a place decidedly not designed or prepared for unofficial transients.

Having completed all official chores at the base, I began to think strictly in terms of "Universal Time" (sometimes called Greenwich Mean Time, and written as a 4 digit number of hours and minutes followed by a "Z," spoken "Zulu"). I was planning to arrive at the North Pole at 2400 Z, the moment that the sun would be over the International Date Line. If I assumed a ground speed of 120 knots, that meant departing Eureka at 1900 Z for the 600 nautical mile flight to the pole.

There were several reasons that made this particular timing desirable. My flight track would follow 86° west longitude, not far from 90 degrees. I would thus arrive at the pole with the sun directly off my left wing. The most important reason for arranging this situation was that then the sextant would be most effective in telling me how far I was drifting to the left (west) or right (east) of course as I was approaching the pole. With only one celestial body, the sun, as reference, that was really all I could expect the sextant to do for me. I could determine a "line of position," that is, a line somewhere along which I was located at the time of the solar observation. I wanted that line to be my intended course in crossing the pole. And, because the line of position is always oriented at right angles to the bearing of the celestial body in question, I planned to arrange to have the sun at a bearing of 90 degrees to my heading while crossing the pole. With the sextant I'd be able to determine that line to within about five miles, close enough for me.

As to my actual position along this line (namely my course), I relied heavily on knowing the precise groundspeed. But this I felt I could determine very accurately by timing the crossing of several fjords, and finally the arctic coastline which lay precisely 150 nautical miles to the north of Eureka in 82° 30' north latitude. Given the stable arctic atmosphere, I felt that the extrapolation to the pole would be accurate to within about 10 miles. Besides, I planned to determine many lines of position with the sextant on my way to the pole. And while none of these would yield position fixes as such, they would rapidly show any inconsistency between expectation and reality.

Apart from the navigational advantage of this timing arrangement, I would have the sun to my left-rear during the flight to the pole. This would allow me to use the astrocompass at will, there would be no need for constant squinting into the sun, and the solar illumination of the panorama would be direct, and could be expected to be magnificent. After crossing the pole, on my way to Spitsbergen, the movement of the sun across the sky would again be the same, advancing from the left-rear to a position off my left wing on arrival at Longyearbyen. The reason was that my route entailed a change in direction of 78° to the right, at the pole, for the flight to Spitsbergen. According to plan I would arrive at Longyearbyen airport at seven in the morning, local time— a good time, I thought.

It was 1700 Z when the helicopter mechanic drove me the half mile from the Eureka compound to my airplane. Somewhere enroute between Resolute and Eureka I'd lost my second, and only spare drag funnel to my HF antenna. With me at the antenna reel in the cabin, the mechanic, crawling under the fuselage, attached a small but tough plastic cup to the end of the antenna wire, a last chore before departure.

I started the engine and called the Eureka radio operator, saying I was ready to taxi. She immediately asked the operator of a piece of gravel compacting equipment to clear the runway as I negotiated some loose gravel and ruts toward the more compacted runway surface. At the end of the runway I faced the mile-long strip with a slight downhill grade, wondering how well this tiny bird would fly with 153 gallons— over 900 pounds— of fuel on board. I slowly advanced the throttle, and the airplane was already moving at about 50 knots when the power lever reached the full power stop. I held a slight back pressure on the control wheel to take some weight off the landing gear, and finally added ten degrees of flaps for added lift as the wheels left the ground. Fully airborne and slowly climbing I retracted the wheels, holding the wings very level— no sudden maneuvers now. Eureka called and said that

I "lifted off at 5-9 (1759 Z)," an hour earlier than planned. But that was good enough.

To my left was Slidre Fjord, to my right, slowly rising terrain between two ridges, with crests spaced by 10 miles and each well over 2000 feet high. The rising terrain itself crested in a kind of pass at about 2000 feet some ten miles due north of the airport. Would the airplane be able to climb fast enough to clear that pass without first gaining altitude over the fjord? With just comfortable margins it appeared that it would, and I therefore turned directly to a heading of true north. The rounded gravelly slopes, interspersed very occasionally by drab green patches were bathed in the peaceful golden rays of the arctic sun. A small stream was flowing beneath through the stony desert toward the fjord behind. Soon the tan-colored, rounded ridge ahead began to fall away below, and a fantastic panorama opened ahead.

The northern reaches of Ellesmere Island, sometimes called Grantland, are a cold paradise of fjords. Long tongues of water cut and angle ever deeper into the rugged, mountainous ice-desert land. Silent glacier mountains stand in rounded rows until the last is lost over the horizon. Peak after peak, and ridge after ridge take on an ever deeper tint of pastel peach or blue in their silent, rigid march to the horizon. The color of this upper surface of an ice-blanket seemed to be very sensitive to the feeble shading provided by occasional thin streaks of cloud overhead. The thick, stretched pancake-like ice blankets terminate in rounded edges that have a crystalline quality. Like crystal, they take on and refract the dominant color of the rock they overlie and whose fragments they incorporate. In the distance to my right was an edge of glassy, dark reddish brown. Small streams arise in the stoney rubble at the edges of the glaciers and spill over the gravel to the far ends of fjords.

But not all of the terrain, or even the rounded mountain heights are covered with ice. About half of the land is simply a gravel-covered mountainscape, crumbling bedrock, interrupted everywhere by sometimes deviously winding fjords.

To my left-front was the junction of Eureka and Nansen Sounds, which form the channel between Axel Heiberg and Ellesmere Islands, with Greely Fjord, which cuts deeply into Ellesmere Island. These drawn-out waterways, here about 12 to 18 miles across, were of a sky blue, with an occasional massive iceberg laying on the surface. The icebergs, brilliant white on top, shone an emerald green on their vertical faces, a color both mirrored in, and arising from beneath the water. A slab of drift ice with rounded edges appeared on Eureka Sound, as more of its length emerged from behind the ridge on my left. Nansen Sound appeared to be ice covered in the far distance, a milky blue color. This ice was probably continuous with the ice of the Arctic Ocean into which Nansen Sound opens.

As I continued to climb, I reached and then crossed the entrance to Greely Fjord, which curved away to the right with branching fjords that cut deep valleys both north and south. In the far distance to the east emerged ice mountains of enormous extent, the Agassiz Ice Cap, with many rounded peaks undulating along the horizon, some reaching to 7500 feet. Off to my left, across Eureka Sound, and some 50 miles away appeared the Müller Ice Cap on Axel Heiberg Island.

The northern shoreline of Greely Fjord, and its extension on the northeastern shore of Nansen Sound, fell steeply to the sea and reached 2500 feet within a mile of the water. By this time I'd reached 4500 feet of altitude and decided to level off. Looking to the northwest, I thought I could see the edge of the Arctic Ocean, but the northern end of Nansen Sound was veiled in a light blue-gray mist and I couldn't be sure. I crossed Hare

Fjord, which was almost ice-free, and in 81° N latitude crossed another mountain ridge with a crest of 3000 feet. As I neared this ridge, the valley of Otto Fjord on the other side came into view. My attention suddenly became fixed on the water as the receding crest opened the view of a surface densely covered with rectangular and cube-shaped icebergs, the first time I'd seen anything of the kind. The fjord's surface was blue, but I saw no emerald edges of the bergs reflected in the water. Then I noticed what seemed to be a pattern of white spoondrift on the water, and realized that I was looked at an ice surface. Why should two fjords spaced by less than five miles have such different characters?

Looking off to my right toward the head of Otto Fjord I saw the answer. The large glacier field of the mountain ridge that forms the backbone of Grantland funnelled a broad ice-tongue down the extended valley of the fjord right out into the water. This was obviously a fast moving glacier tongue with an actively calving front, and was still in the process of lengthening the fjord. I was amazed to see two very different colors of rocky slopes on the two sides of the valley forming the funnel; the southern slope was charcoal gray, whereas the one on the north was a reddish tan, which was the most common color of these rocky hills.

Now came the last substantial landmass before the Arctic Ocean; some 50 miles of mountainous terrain with many crests of 4000 feet. The round numbers on the chart struck me as an indication that this land may not have been surveyed in any great detail. But lovely land it was! Remote and untouched, it held forth a majestic aspect. Reason said that this rugged stone desert in mountain relief must be approached with respect. But the warm earth colors and rounded peaks and ridges gave it an alluring and deceptively friendly quality.

I often found myself flying a few hundred feet above long and winding and suddenly descending glacier tongues, wrapped around ridges and over cliffs, flowing to the edges of frozen lakes. In shallow descent the glacier surfaces were smooth, but when the descent angle abruptly increased the glacier became deeply crevassed. Long, fjord-like tongues of water wound through deep valleys, their surfaces rigid with wave-like and intricately scalloped designs of white on a frozen, blue-green background. At other times small tracts of hilly desert passed below. At one point, three neighboring hills had three entirely distinct colors: rust, light tan and charcoal gray.

A small lake, several desert valley streams, another ice-capped peak, and I was approaching Phillips Inlet in 82° N latitude. There was now no mistaking the Arctic Ocean about ten miles to the northwest. The high-relief terrain gave way to the widest and loneliest flat expanse I'd ever seen. But there was nothing obviously different in the surface covering—certainly it was unlike any ocean or other sheet of water I'd ever seen— it was simply white, but obviously solid. It was as though I were looking down from the slopes of a mountain range and out over an unending white plain. But no plain had ever appeared so flat and so wide!

Keeping to my straight line course, I overflew a final peninsula and headed out, over this ice-plain. I was approaching the last point of land I'd see on this side of the Arctic Ocean, called Alert Point (not to be confused with the outpost "Alert"), in 82° 30' North. For 15 miles I was flying over shore ice, five miles from land. The low land was to my right, and a couple of miles to the left I saw the junction of the active pack with the relatively fixed and stationary shore-ice. The junction was simply a narrow, open lead, which, like all other leads of the ice-pack was an irregular jagged line of black ocean water. The shore-ice had no uniform character. Near its junction with the active pack it consisted of floes seemingly permanently welded together; the floes that made up this closed surface could be identified by their individual shadings of light brown-gray, indicating their different ages and origins. Close in to shore this ice had been pressed into a wavy, washboard surface. This was obvious, even from 5000 feet because the white ice surface was interrupted by a series of parallel, drawn-out melt pools of bright aquamarine and blue hues. Where land-ice reached beyond the coastline the surface ice appeared massive, much crevassed and blocky.

Such was the case minutes later as I was passing Alert Point, which is a spreading glacier field flowing from the land, with glacier ice abutting sea ice. Looking back, I saw the last rugged land, jagged lines of rough blue-gray and tan cliffs encased in a world of ice.

Ahead, in all directions, lay the surface of another world, a white world. But white was simply the universal backdrop for a game played by the oblique radiation of the sun with the atmosphere and water. Visibility was without limit, and the air was absolutely calm. Yet the horizon was diffuse, caused by extremely thin filaments of mist snaking into the atmosphere from the sliver-like openings between ice-floes. Because of the low angle of the sun, about 24° above the horizon, these distant mists often took on soft, pastel hues. The infinite sky above was of a soft, peaceful blue, crossed here and there by thin, diffusely edged streaks of high cirrus.

Everywhere, except in the far distance approaching the horizon, the arctic ocean plain was clearly visible and bright. It's solid-looking surface offered a certain deceptive security. But an unusual ice-surface it was. The floes were everywhere covered with round and oblong small patches of bright aquamarine colors. Perhaps a third of the total area was of these colored jewels seemingly inlaid on the white surface. They could only be melt pools formed on the upper surface of the ice. They seemed to be of a reasonably uniform bright blue-green hue, but an occasional one was of a deeper blue. These colors arise because all ice surfaces, including those at the pool bottoms, reflect all wavelengths of sunlight roughly equally. But the water of the pools preferentially absorbs the longer wavelengths— the reds and oranges and yellows, as the light-rays are transmitted through its bulk. The deeper blue of some pools simply spoke of their greater depth.

The entire surface of the ocean was covered with floes. The junctions between neighboring floes constitute lanes or channels of black open water, which often showed how closely the two facing floe edges fit together, so that it was obvious that the two floes in question were once a single floe that had cracked along a ragged line. But sometimes the two edges were not so well matched. This occurred especially near junctions of three lanes. There, indeed, were found pieces of ice of all sizes packed in such a way as to nearly cover the somewhat triangular opening. These leads and open water spaces appeared jet-black to me. They simply absorbed all light that fell on their surfaces. The contrast between white, bright aquamarine and black, each with their unique surface patterns and relative dominance was as pleasing to the eye as it was unexpected.

To these patterns of color must be added the pervasive occurrence of pressure ridges. Like folded mountain ranges, these ridges, formed by the pressing edges of floes, are of many ages. As with mountains, the youngest ridges are also the most spectacular. Typically they form enormously long ridge-lines, crossing the icescape as long leads do. Often, however, they bunch together to form fields of ridges like certain mountainous areas on earth. Then, individual ridges continue on into the distance, crossing with other ridges as they go. From my viewpoint at 5000 feet, these ridge patterns resembled the patterns of trails often left behind on the plains by great animal herd migrations; stringy paths crossing, converging, diverging and clustering.

Pressure ridges may be thrown up in minutes by the ice packing. In the course of days, however, ice packing centers change location on the surface, and old ridges may collapse into lanes as the ice slackens, or they may simply wear away by wind erosion and surface melting, or even rain. Their remnants can often be seen as ice dikes along blue-green surface melt pools.

Forty-five minutes after passing Alert Point, and 110 miles from the nearest arctic coast, with the distance from land ever increasing, it occurred to me to write down a description of what unfolded before me, as it was unfolding. The following quotes from that written log perhaps describe best the advance to the pole and beyond, to my first sighting of Spitsbergen:

"The Arctic Ocean in 84° North [latitude], 86° W longitude, 2000 Z: Finely fractured eggshell. Floes of all sizes, pure white with bright aquamarine pools with rounded edges, the larger ones with irregular but still rounded edges— I assume these are surface melt pools. Cracks in the ice in all directions, but perhaps a preferred direction at about right angles to my course. These cracks are [black in color]. The surface reminds me of solar [surface] photographs [taken of the single hydrogen-alpha spectral line]. Much "brash" in many of the broader leads, brash consisting of chunks of floe and pieces of ice of all sizes. Sometimes there are long leads with abruptly changing directions. Occasionally there are clusters of bright aquamarine pools of all sizes. But the pools are everywhere, and so are the leads.

"Occasionally there are almost oval-shaped areas of light brownish gray surface [about the dimensions of a typical floe]. But generally all of the pool and lead phenomena are on a pure white background which very occasionally changes to an elliptical light gray area." These darker areas are probably of somewhat older ice than their surroundings. The brown-gray color is due to either mineral dust from the atmosphere, or the blooming of a red alga. Nansen found both forms on the ice during the drift of the Fram.

"So far the surface has been 100% visible— no fog on the Ellesmere coast or over the ocean. Bright sunshine initially over Ellesmere and the ocean, but a half hour later had a diffuse overcast. Took an astrocompass reading at 83° N before the overcast obscured the sun. The overcast is now disappearing with blue sky ahead, but it looks from here as though there might be low stratus or fog ahead— the sun seems to be illuminating fog banks in the far distance. ... (2019 Z) I already see thin filaments of stratus or fog on my left over a dark lead ... The sky will be clear again ahead (2021 Z)— should be near 85° N.

"(2023 Z) Very thin wisps of fog below, recognizable over the dark openings. I have no fear over engine failure— this surface seems almost inviting. Plate tectonics (ice plate tectonics) on a finely gridded scale [is occurring there]. I'd have no qualms about putting the airplane down on a larger floe between aquamarine pools [if that were necessary because of a serious emergency]. My exposure suit is next to me as protection against the cold and slush [which one would certainly find there]. Actually the temperature at 5300 feet of altitude is now 3+° C (2128 Z).

"Complex pattern of aquamarine pools below just now (2129 Z) and many broader intersecting leads. Very wispy stratus below. The sunlit edge of the surface [is] just ahead now. Should have passed 85° N (2031 Z). Will take another sun shot in a few minutes.

"No land in sight anywhere, although visibility is easily 100 miles in all directions. Thin rolls of low clouds far below looking toward the sun (7:30 o'clock position). 2033 Z."

The sight of this reflecting "fog bank" in the general direction of the sun was a surprising observation, because, viewed from any other direction, these low mists were virtually transparent. In a related connection, Payer expresses himself as follows ([6], p324, my translation): "In fact its not a rare occurrence in arctic regions that the mist-banks of the horizon take on the definite character of distant lines of hills, because the low elevation to which the vapors are capable of rising in the cold air causes their sharp delineation; most often this misidentification takes the form of distant out-flows of enormous glaciers." ...

"I now see pressure ridges, intersecting (or running in all directions). They look like mountain ranges on a relief map ... 2035 Z 85+° N latitude.

"Aquamarine pools, black lanes and [jagged] openings, and pressure mounds (hummocks) everywhere. The [low] sun illuminates the pressure mounds to make them brilliant white on one side and shady white on the other. The pressure mounds and ridges are far more pronounced now, and the dark open leads shorter, but everything is very numerous. 2044 Z.

"The airplane [is] behaving well, the autopilot is flying— the air is very smooth— 5300 feet [of altitude] hands off for at least 45 minutes now. The pattern of pressure ridges looks like trails of migrating animals, crisscrossing and clustered in places in the middle near distance. 2048 Z." The autopilot held the wings level and was coupled to the directional gyro to hold a set heading. It did not sense or hold altitude.

"Almost 3 hours under way. Must give Resolute Bay a position report in a few minutes on the HF radio: 86° N, 86° W. Ice floes very broken up locally just here (2049 Z)."

I attempted to give a position report via short wave radio every two degrees of latitude, or about every hour. The sole purpose of these reports was to limit the search area for rescue flights if I failed to show up at the other end. When I asked the personnel at Eureka about possible modes of rescue for a downed aircraft on a flight such as this, they told me that if the downing occurred within 300 miles of Eureka, they'd send one of their two helicopters to pick me up. If it happened farther out, Resolute would probably dispatch a Twin Otter on skis. I had also been informed that the Canadians had an agreement with the Russians to use several Soviet satellites to monitor the arctic areas for any ELT (Emergency Locator Transmitter) transmissions from downed aircraft. All of this sounded very reassuring, but I sincerely hoped that the efficacy of these measures would not have to be put to the test. In fact, unless my ELT batteries (which maintain charge for about two hours of transmitting) held out, there was virtually no chance that I would ever be found in this vast emptiness.

Regarding my intention to give position reports I actually lost all radio contact for over four hours. I knew that short wave radio worked poorly over the Arctic Ocean. I explained that to myself by theorizing that with the geomagnetic field lines oriented almost vertically in that region, there was probably no ionosphere overhead which, when present, refracts the skywave of HF radio signals, allowing for their propagation around the earth's curving surface.

"Sextant gives 21° 24' sun altitude at 2115 Z, 86° 30' N, 86° W. Appear to be right on course— probably no more than 5 miles off. 2118 Z."

This guess of 5 miles was based on an interpolation among precomputed solar bearings (called Zn) and altitudes (Hc), for July 25, at 83, 85, 87 and 89 degrees N latitude along the 8 6° W meridian, for the anticipated times over those locations. A later, more accurate calculation showed that the solar altitude for the stated position and time was 21°39', which means that my actual position was on a line parallel to, and some 15 nautical miles to the northeast of my estimated line-of-position. One of the annoyances of navigating by the stars is that it is easier to calculate the altitude for an assumed position, than it is to measure the altitude and to compute the corresponding line-of-position, that is, to do the inverse calculation. Thus, in practice, navigation is by a form of trial-and-error rather than by direct deductive reasoning; this last, the concept of "sight-reduction" would suggest. Fortunately, these things simplify in the immediate vicinity of the pole (within 40 or 50 miles), and it would be easier to make final course corrections there.

"2119 Z. Still the same aquamarine pools, dark lanes and pools, pressure ridge patterns, and so it will probably be right up to the pole. Beautiful weather, high scattered cirrus, horizon slightly hazy, no fog or stratus— actually *unbelievable*. (The thin fog filaments earlier seem to have been associated with the overcast I had then— nothing of the kind now.) 2123 Z.

"It feels like evening— I suppose because of the position of the sun (and also its dimming due to the cirrus). Looking toward the sun, the surface is intricately patchy, reflecting (but not blinding). I suppose the summer melt pools are reflecting. The remaining background surface looks dull in comparison."

Even as I was completing these sentences, it occurred to me that this supposition was probably wrong. The glistening

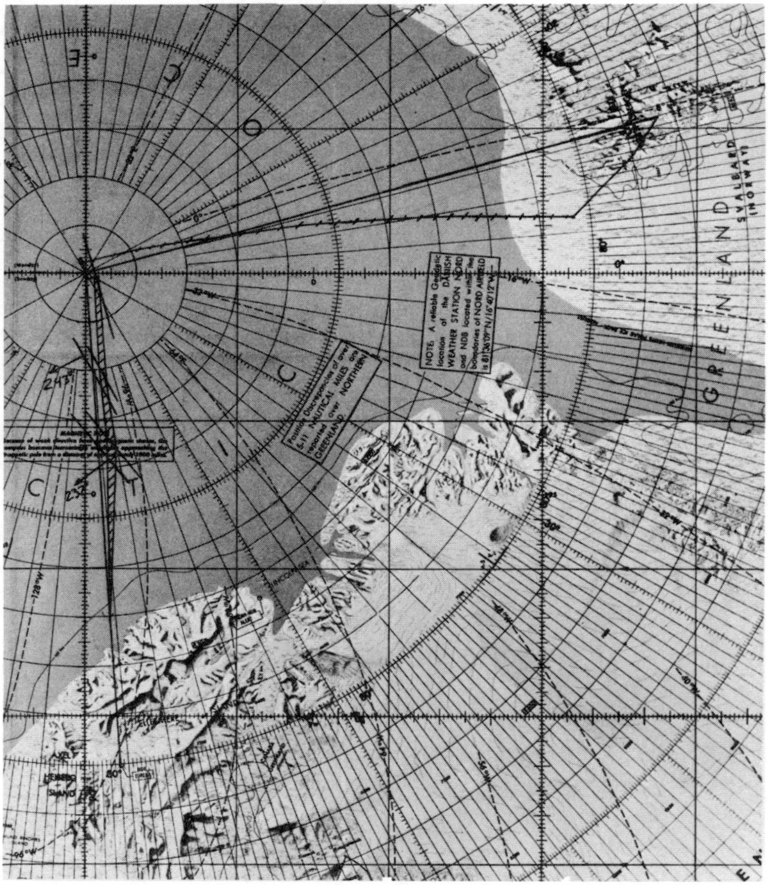

Flight track (crosshatched) over the Arctic Ocean.

area was far too extensive for all of it to be sufficiently aligned to mirror the sun. The sparkling was probably due to the reflection and refraction from the myriad of minute and randomly oriented ice crystals of the slushy floes. And it was the melt pools that provided the closely spaced dull "holes" in the sparkle. I confirmed this later when I was flying at about 50 feet above the pressure ridges and saw innumerable prismatic shafts of light randomly flashing over the ice surface. The effect was similar to that observed when walking across a powder snow-field on a bright, sunny day. The melt pools, in contrast, appeared as still lagoons from up close.

"2127 Z. In 87° N latitude now, aiming straight at the pole. The magnetic compass is reading 145°, absolutely ridiculous, but of course it is the [magnetic] variation and in that it is right on. When I make my 79° right turn at the pole I suppose that the compass will read magnetic south [180 degrees] because there is very little variation on my way to Spitsbergen."

According to my chart (GNC-1) the magnetic variation almost all of my way to the pole should have been about 115°W. I discounted the 30° discrepancy on the basis of "compass unreliability," preferring to rely on the accuracy of the position of the sun. The chart variation on the route from the pole to Spitsbergen declines from 10°W near the pole, to about 0° at Spitsbergen.

"It's amazing! I'm over the Arctic Ocean, dead reckoning with astrocompass and sextant. I feel *exhilarated,* no hint of fear. Totally confident that Svalbard will appear right on schedule. But, of course, the weather is so beautiful, just a minute trace of hazy layers. Autopilot still flying; I've corrected the DG only 10 degrees [to the west]. Altitude stable at 5330 feet (29.92" Hg). Temperature, 3° C." 29.92 inches of mercury (Hg) is the standard atmospheric pressure at the surface. The aircraft altimeter is set for standard pressure when there is no weather reporting station nearby to give the actual local barometric pressure.

"Position report to Radio Alert: Time 2153 Zulu, 88 North, 86 West, estimating the pole at 2250 Zulu.

"Alert relayed [this] position to Resolute Bay. Resolute apparently unable to read me. The North Pole in less than an hour! 2159 Z.

"Sextant gives 20° 12.5' @ 2200 Z.

"2226 Z. Am flying at an altitude of only about 50 feet to see the lanes, ridges and hummocks at close hand (89° N). The altimeter is actually reading below sea level (-50 feet)— I suppose it's the high pressure I'm in. Temperature 0° C. No problem to get down unharmed [if I should have a sudden engine failure], but the airplane would be broken.

"Sextant reads 19° 10' (2238 Z). I'm within 20 miles of the pole!

"Sextant altitude 19° 23' (2244Z). I'm within 5 miles of the pole!

"Position, 2255 Zulu, 90° North (North Pole). Estimating Longyearbyen, Svalbard 0450 Z."

Although I transmitted this position report on 5680 kHz I received no acknowledging response. But that troubled me not in the least. I was in the highest of spirits. For the moment the pole was mine alone. How wonderful, I thought, that nature had arranged the North Pole to be in the middle of a dynamic ice ocean. All attempts to put up cairns and flags would be swept away. There was no danger of this pole losing its pristine character. We may occasionally intrude, fleetingly, but nature would reclaim her domain and remove all our symbols of "conquest."

To allow for possible errors in the position timing based in part on dead reckoning, I decided to fly for 10 minutes beyond the calculated position of the pole. That way I'd be sure to have crossed it, as there was no clue to the pole's position from anything to be seen on the surface. The surface was that of the Arctic Ocean described earlier, except that the entire area within a few degrees of latitude (a couple hundred miles) of the North Pole seemed particularly densely packed with ice. Pressure ridges abounded, as did surface melt pools, but all open leads were short and very narrow; sliver-like.

During those 10 minutes I took three sextant altitudes. They all fell within five minutes of arc of the solar declination, which was N 19° 27'. But I also wanted to see and observe everything, the ice, the atmosphere. I looked down and to the horizon and at the sky. Why did I come here? A friend once said to me that she thought of me when she read about the flyby of Uranus by Voyager. Well, it was impossible to fly to Uranus, but there was the North Pole. And I was a child longing for adventure, for the majesty of remote nature, and to remove myself — if only for a short while — from the hubbub of dense humanity with its pride and moral posturing and subtle coercion to join the herd.

At 2257 Z I turned 180 degrees to backtrack for a few minutes, and wrote:

"How easy, it's amazing! I'm not tired at all! Quite the contrary— I feel like I could fly forever! Wispy, hazy atmosphere at 5000 feet. But in most directions I can see the horizon very clearly ..."

As I was banked to the left during the slow half-circle turn I had a natural drawn-out scan of this expansive ice-field. The thin, transparent hazyness imparted a somewhat sombre quality — a recent change — to the scenery. The sun was still shining, but its oblique light seemed diminished in the pale blue sky and in the absence of the earlier brightness from the oceanic plain of ice with its innumerable still lagoons. Two minutes later I made a careful turn to a heading for Svalbard; it would be some five hours before I'd reach that glaciated archipelago.

"The pole is just behind me (2259 Z), on my way to Spitsbergen. Will take the astrocompass down because the sun is directly behind me and I can't get a reading for a while now. The surface is just as before. I've still got 30 gallons in the ferry tank, full mains [wing tanks]. I really do have over 16 hours range! ... 2500 mile range, great. I could easily go all the way to [mainland] Norway and then some [if the local weather prevented a landing on Spitsbergen]."

Shortly after leaving the immediate vicinity of the pole I began to encounter sagging overcast clouds. These arctic clouds had no clearly defined edges that I could see. Imperceptibly the pale blue of the sky changed to a light gray. Ahead, the clouds were a darker gray, and the shade of their diffuse bases merged continuously with the drab shade of the ice surface of the ocean. Payer writes that "the cloudforms in the realm of the ice-ocean never take on the sharp contours of those in more southern latitudes ..." I couldn't tell whether I'd have to descend to stay out of the clouds. But even if I did have to descend to remain clear, I felt that it wouldn't be by more than a couple thousand feet. Still, I was 450 miles from the nearest arctic coast (the northernmost cape of Greenland, which is also the most northern point of land on earth), and I cast many glances at the thermometer. But the temperature held steady above freezing.

I passed the first stretch of dark overcast, and some brighter strips of sunlit surface emerged in the distance ahead. I relaxed a little. But the same situation would occur again and again, and the sunlit surface strips were all too fleeting. At the lowest points of the overcasts I'd be forced down to about 4000 feet of altitude. But, in truth, my spirits were so high that all pessimistic thoughts were blocked out of my mind. Far from wishing for an airfield, I was saddened at the thought of this flight ending. For the first time I was glad that mine was not a very fast airplane.

"2350 Z. Navigation by dead reckoning! I have the airplane pointed south after making a 79° right turn. Solar navigation not possible at the present time ... Hazy to my left front with a wispy, diffuse, almost translucent overcast. But it looks like it will be clear up ahead again soon.

"This flight is going much too fast! It seems as though it will be over before I can fully grasp it. I was a little anxious, just before takeoff. All that seems total folly now. The Arctic Ocean is all around— nothing else in sight. It is a vast expanse of ice, and yet it will all be over so quickly. But when I think of Nansen and others walking and sledding across it— they had a long way to go. I imagine to myself what it would be like to make this trip floe by floe, lane after lane. The pressure ridges and hummocks don't seem so bad [actually, the sheer number of them seemed formidable for any extended journey], at least not this time of year, but the surface is probably very bad to ski and sled over [actually, it was probably impossible to ski and sled over]. It sure is pretty from up here. Looks like an enormous, cracked egg shell of some exotic bird [an eggshell intricately spotted with aquamarine patches, random, stringy ridges, and cracked along black leads].

"0003 Z. Magnetic compass reads 209°, which would mean a 29° West variation [assuming that the directional gyro was correctly set. I was flying by the DG on a heading of 180 degrees, and did not yet trust the magnetic compass sufficiently to navigate by it]. I expected a substantial [magnetic] variation at the pole, but it should be down a little by now. It should be about 0° at Spitsbergen. If the DG is off I'll come down a little too far west. Oh well, we'll see in a few hours, and I'll be flying into an area of Loran coverage, so it will be all right. I do have a fluffy, variable overcast now, though. I wonder what the weather will be at Spitsbergen. Again (or still) at about 5600 feet of altitude."

"0011 Z. This is certainly the most comfortable way to undertake a polar expedition! Still have almost 30 gallons in the ferry tank [in reality, this was certainly closer to 20 gallons]— full mains. Flying by the Global Navigation Chart (GNC-1).

"0053 Z. Can no longer make contact on the HF [radio]; haven't been able to for a while. Grayish overcast, but strips of sunlight ahead. The surface is of large floes with innumerable aquamarine pools on each, but the floes are separated by what Nansen would have called the ugliest of lanes (from the point of view of surface travel). Some floes are neatly cracked, and some show the remnants of old pressure ridges. It got a little bumpy all of a sudden, but then I've felt a few bumps earlier, always at the point of lowest overcast, which however is well above 5000 feet, probably diffuse ceiling of 8000. [This was an optimistic estimate. The lowest ceilings were a little under 5000 feet.]

"0059 Z. Clearing ahead with some high clouds. Temperature, 4° C.

"0101 Z. I keep thinking that I see fog banks on the distant surface ahead. I do so now, but so far it's always turned out to be strips of surface sunshine. The surface is perfectly clear, and of the forms described.

"0104 Z. My mind is getting pretty mushy in its time sense. Things ([time, and] latitude lines) seem to be going by so quickly. [This was written about half an hour after eating my sandwich and I think that the effects of digestion in conjunction with the always-present vibrations had something to do with this feeling.] But the instruments (fuel flow gauge, watch, ferry tank sight gauge) all agree as to the distance travelled. To be honest, I really don't know where I am, but the [apparent] magnetic variation has come down some (comparing compass with DG suggests 20° W variation). But, on the other hand, I haven't touched the DG in hours, and I have no idea [but nevertheless, some suspicion] whether it's drifted some or not. My earlier experience suggests that it's quite stable.

"0109 Z. The sun is coming out again, and a welcome companion it is. Temperature is down to 3° C (1° down from earlier) suggesting some slight difference in the air mass, but perhaps it's only that I'm slightly higher now (4820 feet, 29.92" Hg)." I had been down to about 4200 feet to remain clear of the latest low point in the overcast.

I was now flying into an arctic wonderland. Large clouds were everywhere, but they now formed more separated cloud streets. Their edges were still diffuse, but now at least identifiable. These diffuse edges softly radiated wonderful pastel pink and peach sunlight. Illuminated obliquely, these colors blended beautifully with the soft lilac and blues of the shaded ice ocean surface, which was now becoming slightly foggy. Presently, the edge of an extensive undercast would appear, adding its own distinctive structural pattern to the panorama. Softly tinted streaks of cirrus were drifting high in the pale blue sky between the shifting perspective of the layered cloud streets.

Just before departing the pole I had carefully set the DG by the astrocompass. The DG seemed to be stable in long straight-line flight, but I wasn't sure that it didn't drift transiently right after the turn at the pole. Because of the later magnetic compass readings I suspected that the DG had indeed drifted by 10 to 15 degrees. But there was no way to check that with the astrocompass because to use that compass would have required turning the airplane to make the sun, which was directly behind me, accessible to the compass sights; and such turning was the suspected cause of drifting of the DG. A little later, even the option of turning was lost because the sun disappeared behind the overcast.

But if I was coming down a little to the west, that was all right with me. It was on the western side of Svalbard that Loran coverage extended farthest to the north, probably to aid Norwegian whalers. I thus intended to use Loran for a single fix as I came off the Arctic Ocean. This would then preclude the possibility of flying through the large open water gap between the Svalbard Archipelago and Greenland without seeing either one, and then finding myself over the North Atlantic with insufficient fuel to reach a coastline. At about 0200 Z I made a failed attempt to contact Longyearbyen on 5680 kiloHertz. Although radio contact was not established, I suspect that Longyearbyen heard me and tried to answer because, a little later, I was surprised by their radio call to me.

"0112 Z. A huge sunlit icefield from 12:00 to 3:00 o'clock position. Things seem to be clearing well ahead. Will now set up the astrocompass once again.

"0120 Z. Astrocompass suggests that I am coming down about 13 degrees too far west (or rather, my heading is 13° too far west). That would tally well with the variation.

"0122 Z. Now the fog banks have arrived— this time it was no illusion. I'm trading an overcast for a low stratus deck. But the surface is still visible between the rolls of fog.

"0132 Z. Ferry tank fuel is just disappearing from the sight gauge; I've been flying 7-1/2 hours now. Should have passed 85° N latitude.

"0135 Z. Fog banks to the horizon, but [looking] straight down the surface is still visible through the rolls. For the moment, blue sky and sunshine over my left shoulder; the fog banks seem to be in the shade again ahead.

"0153 Z. Estimating 84° N, 005° E. The scenery is so soft— low, soft-looking stratus or fog below— soft, pastel streaks of clouds high in the sky— somewhat more dense cloud streets overhead— the sun is illuminating patchy areas of the fog in all directions. Have not had meaningful HF contact in a long time. Just gave a position report, but I don't know who to, or if it was copied; it was to some station that I could hear briefly and that acknowledged my identification numbers. The engine seems to be rumbling with my headset on over the bows of my sunglasses. It's very quiet with earplugs on (when I have them on).

"0206 Z. I can see the pack ice through the lower fog layer. It consists of floes of all sizes, true floes and ice cakes of all sizes. The aquamarine color [of the melt pools] is not to be distinguished (or barely distinguished) through the fog, shaded as it is now by a diffuse higher cloud street.

"I've seen no real polynjas yet, but some of the irregular openings are becoming larger."

A polynja (a Russian word) is a relatively large area of water formed among the arctic pack ice and kept open almost continuously by strong surface currents of the sea. They occur in the vicinity of arctic lands, particularly if relatively narrow sea channels, sounds or basins are nearby.

"0211 Z. A very large floe off to my left, so far as I can make out through the fog.

"0215 Z. Amazing, Longyearbyen just called and came in quite clear. I gave position report, and he gave me some good news on the weather— better than 10 miles visibility. The fog below is also quite thin at the moment, exposing all of the features of that unique Arctic Ocean. The ice pack is much looser now than over the pole. Is it the effect of winds and drift and the ice edge to the south? 0223 Z.

"0227 Z. Beautiful sharp horizon on my right, extending

from 1 o'clock [position] right around to the back. No sharp horizon [is to be seen] in the other directions. Or, if there is a sharp line as there is at my 7 to 8 o'clock position, I cannot tell whether it's horizon or a stratus edge.

"0257 Z. Loran has been initialized for [the] Norwegian Sea Chain grid, has picked up signals from Y and Z slaves, is searching for master signal. Pack ice obscured more or less by fog and stratus. Beautiful clear sky ahead, with the same soft, dreamy tints of the arctic. Should be in 82° N latitude.

"0330 Z. Spitsbergen has been in sight for some time. Open water below."

Approaching the west coast of Spitsbergen.

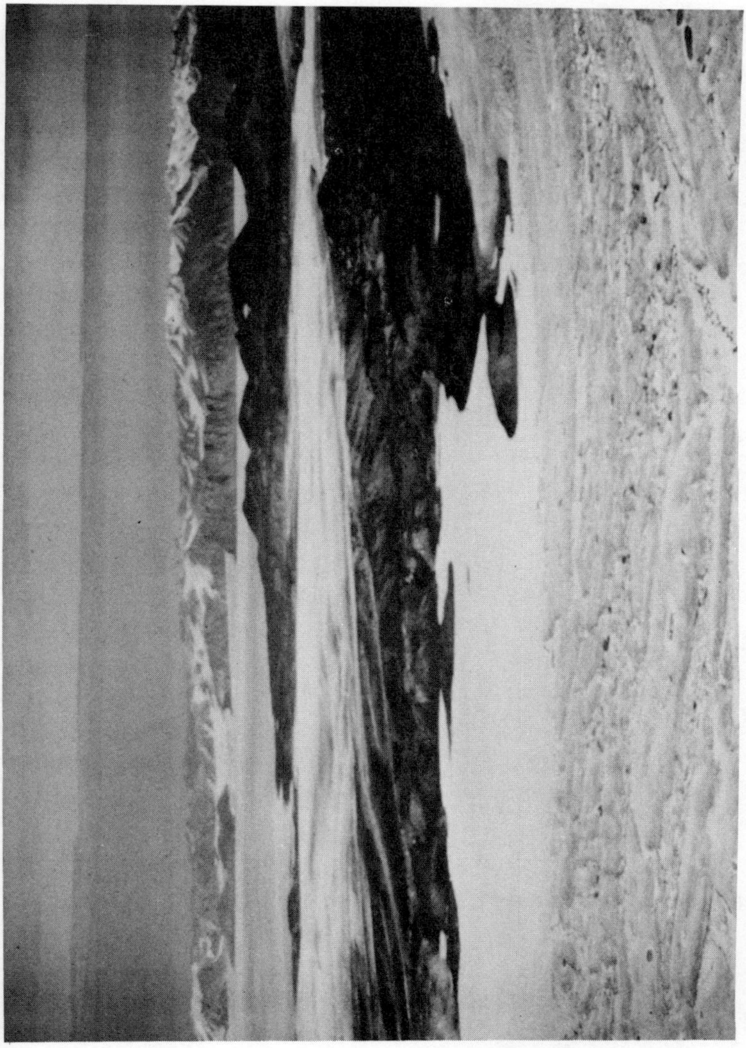

Alert Point on Grantland, Ellesmere Island; the last land facing the Arctic Ocean.

Sketchmap of the Svalbard Archipelago.

Chapter 5

SVALBARD, AND THE BARENTS AND NORWEGIAN SEAS

At 0315 Z on July 26 I thought that I should be approaching 81° North latitude. The main island of Spitsbergen extends a small point of land, Mosselhalvøya (Mossel's peninsula), above the 80th degree of latitude. Farther east, Nordaustlandet (Northeastland), the second largest island of the Svalbard Archipelago, reaches to 80° 30' N, with a cluster of islets, Sjuøyane (Seven Islands), breaking the surface of the sea as far north as 80° 48'. Therefore, I could expect land to come in sight at any time.

Instinctively, I looked to the horizon on the left-front and saw a sharp and jagged line. An instant later I recognized mountainous land emerging from the distant mist in the 10 o'clock direction and forming the horizon from there to about 11:30 o'clock. Although this azimuthal range is not large, the land seemed quite extensive to me because of its distance. In hue it differed very little from the misty atmosphere in that direction; it was a light gray-pink. But its intricately angling patterns marked it as land, a long and slender sawblade among a complex collection of clouds, mists and fogs.

Portions of the land seemed to be shaded; but its distant and receding northeastern extremity was of an unending and gleaming glacier-front. Several seemingly conflicting emotions arose in my heart. The loveliness of this scenery triggered boundless joy. The suddenness of the appearance of land, with its promise of salvation, engendered both relief and disappointment simultaneously; disappointment because I had unknowingly looked forward to a search for land, a search that required the application of my own keen powers, and that could be savored for a time. Now I was robbed of that search. And while the presence of land seemed to suggest a haven and safety after a long time of isolated abandonment over a frozen ocean, intruding rational thoughts said that there is nothing kindly about the aspect of this land, and any sense of safety is a cruel illusion.

I looked straight down and saw dark water below; not an ice-floe to be seen anywhere. The surface was of somewhat rounded and closely spaced wave crests and troughs extending in long, parallel rows, with several groups of rows angling in different directions and forming complex grid patterns. I observed this surface and saw the patterns slowly changing. A pair of interacting crests reared up in slow motion, and in the same slow motion spread before them a blanket of white foam. The blanket then dissipated ever so slowly. Now I saw similar phenomena playing out elsewhere on the surface of the sea. The slow motion was, of course, an illusion, and simply spoke of the size of the ocean swells 5000 feet below. The land was still many miles away, and the thought of ditching in this sea after 9-1/2 hours of flight, and with the water temperature near the freezing level, was anything but pleasant.

I again looked around at the atmosphere and found it most magnificent. Perhaps only perfectly clear air would have been as welcome. The pastel edges of higher stratus clouds were diffusely enshrouded by the soft mist in the air. The surface to the north was lost in extensive fog; all attempts to see the edge of the arctic pack ice were in vain. In the direction of the land was the edge of a low layer of altocumulus clouds, casting its shadow onto the surface of the sea. Beyond the low cloud layer were the still distant jagged peaks rising out of the water. The peaks were not high, typically 3000 feet, but the misty dark rock crested everywhere in pointed ridges. Suspended like hammocks between the ridges are long and broad ice-fields reaching to the edge of the sea.

The Loran receiver had now acquired the signals of all stations of the Norwegian Sea Chain. I pushed the receiver button to display present position: N80° 20', E006° 58'. There was now no further question; I was looking at "Albert the First Land" on the island of Spitsbergen. I turned the airplane to a heading of 130 degrees, which was a kind of compromise between the shortest route to land, and a direct heading for Longyearbyen airport. The airport lay just south and west of the geographical center of the island of Spitsbergen on a point of land on the southern shore of the broad and branching Isfjorden (Ice Fjord), which cuts deeply into the island from the west-southwest. I switched on one of my VHF radios and also the ADF (Automatic Direction Finding) receiver and set its frequency to the NDB (Non-Directional Beacon) used as a fix for one of the instrument approaches. The navigation half of the VHF radio I switched to one of the two localizer frequencies. The "localizer" defines lateral displacement from the centerline on an instrument approach. But I was still too far away to receive the signals from either of these radio facilities. Next, I entered in the Loran receiver, as waypoints, the coordinates of the airport and of two approach fixes, "Alpha" and "Bravo." Alpha and Bravo are geographical locations, one north and one south, and each about 10 miles from the airport. The landing rules at Longyearbyen specify that incoming aircraft should report to the control tower over one or the other of these fixes.

I then called the tower operator on HF to give my precise position, and time of arrival, which I estimated to be 0430 Z.

The man in the tower told me of beautiful, clear weather with light winds, and we then entered upon a discussion of the arctic and of Fridtjof Nansen. The topics of radio conversations can go far afield when flying in remote areas with virtually no other traffic of any kind.

I was now approaching the land at a point just south of the small Magdalenefjorden, which is a little south of the northwest corner of Spitsbergen. The sun was directly over the land to the east and the mountain flanks facing the sea were shaded. But the numerous broad glacier fields between the pointed ridges radiated a bronze light at the low solar reflection angle. It was already becoming clear to me that no land is more appropriately named than Spitsbergen. "Pointed Mountain," indeed. The entire surface of western Spitsbergen is that of a giant rasp; pointed ridges cross the landscape in every direction. And the valleys are filled with thick blankets of dynamic ice, gently curving upwards along the mountain flanks, and often exposing the rock only at the pointed mountain peaks.

The small stretch of sea that remained before the glacier and mountain coast was shimmering with the golden rays of the sun. To my right-front was a long ridge of land rising out of the sea parallel to the shoreline of Spitsbergen, Prins Karls Forland. This mountain ridge was covered with glaciers or snow, almost down to the water's edge, where there was a narrow strip of exposed rock. These white mountains caught the direct sunlight, and lay there, still, and surrounded by clear blue sky and sea, a marvelous picture of morning.

As I was about to cross the shore, the Loran receiver, which had been supplying a steady flow of updated navigational data, suddenly announced a "Skywave Warning." I acknowledged the warning with the push of a button, but now the set appeared to be somewhat confused. Distance and groundspeed information varied erratically from one displayed value to the next. And some of the values displayed left more than a reasonable doubt as to their feasibility, to say the least. (The Loran is programmed to calculate and update its data once every five seconds). Another "skywave warning," and before I could acknowledge that one, the Loran switched its message to "Station Search/Settle." I switched the receiver to show the Loran Chain in use. This was still the Norwegian Sea Chain, as expected, but the set had lost the signals from the master and one or two of the slave stations. It struck me that it may be more than coincidence that the receiver began to fail just as I was crossing the shoreline overland. Indeed, I found later that the Loran worked beautifully in crossing the sea from Spitsbergen to Norway, and again later during the Atlantic crossing. But it failed to function over land until I reached the southern tip of Spitsbergen five days later, it failed again just before reaching the Norwegian coast on that flight, and failed yet again as I was approaching Greenland after crossing the Atlantic Ocean.

The failure of the Loran receiver meant simply that I had to rely on more basic modes of navigation, such as looking at the ground. This fit well with my wishes as I crossed Mitra peninsula, which harbors a small frozen lake from which a stream flows down to the sea, and then Krossfjorden. I was now flying parallel to Kongsfjorden just off to the right, and a little farther off to the right the snow covered mountains of Prins Karls Forland were smiling from 20 to 60 miles away.

Beyond the head of Kongsfjorden was a land mass covered almost completely by an ice sheet, but with many isolated rocky points and ridges thrusting up and piercing the glacier. The glacier here must make many devious turns through curving and branching valleys before it straightens its flow in long ice tongues to the edge of the sea. Several of these broad ice-streams were heavily crevassed. Deep, closely spaced grooves crossed the ice surfaces in parallel rows from one side of each valley to the other. Lengthwise, these glaciers showed two strips of a fairly dark greenish brown, so-called *medial moraines,* on the otherwise white upper surface with pale blue, crystal faces into the cracks.

Ahead lay the blue and rippling surface of Isfjorden. It is a rather broad channel of water that terminates in radiating fingers of somewhat narrower fjords. I called the control tower from twenty miles away as I crossed the northern shore over water, and received landing clearance in an easy, off-handed way; there had been no traffic at the airport for hours in this early morning.

Occasional thin and fluffy peach-colored clouds hung over some of the glaciers to the east. The clear and cold surface of Isfjorden was sparkling in the sun, and betrayed its thin aura of bluish mist only along its distant shores where land and glacier-fronts plunged into the sea. The determined frontier-foothold of man — in the form of a distant runway and airport structures — stood on an exposed terrace in a sunflooded landscape of desolate hill-ridges, which responded with a soft visual texture to the perpetual morning light of the arctic summer. Times and distances seemed drawn-out as I glided out over the water and then, five minutes later, savored a wide left turn onto the final approach, landing into the sun. During the rollout I heard the controller's voice in my headset, "Arrival, 4:28 universal time." I could park, I was told, next to the German aircraft on the otherwise empty tarmac.

My actions were deliberate as I slowly and systematically shut down this faithful bird. The compass-rose of the directional gyro began to spin uncontrollably. I "caged" the gyro to prevent possible wear on bearings, and made a mental note to have the instrument inspected. But such a trifle could not affect a whole collection of euphoric feelings. I had never imagined otherwise, but even so, I had actually crossed the Arctic Ocean over the North Pole. I had actually "made it." So it was possible to do after all. I felt fortunate to have had the dream, and to have seen with my own eyes the frozen seas and atmospheres of the extreme north.

I unplugged my headset, and began to fold and order the pile of charts and other debris on the seat next to me. I packed the sextant and astrocompass in their cases, and stowed them along with the Loran, and then climbed over the bag containing the exposure suit, onto the wing and into the cool arctic summer air. I had been airborne for 10-1/2 hours, and I was a little tired. And as I took the first few steps towards the large hangar I felt sharp pains in my lower back. But these soon subsided. Mountain ridges with tinted snowfields on their upper slopes stood in all directions, with a long cliff-face parallel to, and just south of the runway and a sparkling fjord on the other side, with bluegreen glacier-fronts on the shores in the distance.

I was alone on the open expanses of the airport as I walked toward the control tower. The tower operator unlatched the ground-floor entrance with the push of a button from his cab six flights up. And after climbing the stairs I was greeted in a most friendly manner. The Norwegian flag outside, floating on the light breeze with its trailing edge rakishly cut to form three points, and the slight accent in the controller's English and his somewhat noble bearing, were all evidence that I had arrived in Europe; or, in any case, at a Norwegian outpost. I was offered a comfortable chair in this room of windows lined with sloping panels of instruments and tables of weather charts and light-signal guns hanging from the ceiling. At first I declined the offer of a cup of coffee, expecting soon to go to sleep. But as I had no desire for sleep, and because the personnel responsible for the daily operations of the airport, including those of the "Airport Hotel," were not expected for another hour (it was then 7 o'clock in the morning), I finally accepted the coffee. It was like an instant addiction; the flavor of this coffee was glorious, as I remembered it from previous times in Europe. I believe that I nearly emptied this poor controller's pot. But he took no offense at this, and we had an extremely amiable conversation in this room flooded with morning sunshine, until the day's activities began to stir below. My timing had, in fact, been perfect because I can think of no happier way to have spent this first hour after my long flight. And I thank this controller for his conversation and hospitality.

Three days later I was ready to depart, to fly the length of the southern half of Spitsbergen, and to cross the 500 miles of sea to mainland Norway. The people on Spitsbergen had said that this had been an exceptionally beautiful summer, and the weather for the crossing was forecast to be excellent. The flight plan was filed and as I turned the ignition switch, the engine turned over once, and then the starter motor simply whirred and failed to further engage the engine. Problems; serious problems because of the isolation here. The shear pin of the starter motor had sheared. This pin is a very small piece of metal, less than 1/2 inch in its greatest dimension; a safety device, although to me it has always seemed to be an ill-conceived irritant with no possible connection to safety. But its failure allowed me to spend two extra days on the island.

Most of Svalbard is a national park or otherwise protected. Polar bears can be a problem. It is suggested that a rifle be carried when away from Longyearbyen. But under no conditions is one allowed to shoot at a polar bear. There is a clause however; the one exception to this rule is when the bear is about to prepare you for his dinner.

Svalbard is a natural attractor for geologists, and I met several on my walks and in the cafeteria in the village. The islands appear to be uplifted continental shelf of the Eurasian plate. The rocks on the west coast are continuous with those on the northern reaches of Greenland. But the two islands parted company tens of millions of years ago when the North Atlantic Ocean opened, and they are still increasing their distance by an inch or two each year.

About 1200 Norwegians live and work on Svalbard, almost all of them in Longyearbyen. The town is situated along a narrow valley, Adventdalen, near the head of a short fjord. The leading edges of two glacier tongues command the upper end of Adventdalen, and peer down upon the town. Siltladen glacial meltwaters rush down the center of the valley and continually threaten the pilings of bridges, which appear to be on the verge of being swept away. Down by the shore lies a harbor and a number of beach cottages, including that of the local wind-surfing club. Needless to say, all windsurfing is done in wet- and dry-suits. Long, well insulated pipes cross the local landscape above ground on pilings because water and sewage would freeze in underground pipes in the permafrost.

Longyearbyen and the Russian villages of Barentsburg and Pyramiden exist only because of extensive layers of coal under the local geological formation. Except for coal mining, Spitsbergen would be unpopulated. Viking seafarers discovered the island in the 13th century. By longstanding international agreement, Spitsbergen belongs to Norway. But the agreement permits any party from nations that have signed the Svalbard treaty to develop an economic enterprise on the island. Thus, the Russians have constructed Barentsburg and Pyramiden, and have mined coal there since before World War II. There is no road connecting Longyearbyen, Barentsburg or Pyramiden, and the 3000 Russians on the island travel by helicopter to the airport. These red-painted helicopters always fly in pairs, and two days after my arrival there was the monthly renewal of Soviet personnel. A Soviet jetliner dominated the tarmac of the airport as flight after flight of helicopters exchanged personnel with Barentsburg. The engine noise was intense for the hour or so of this process, during which I visited the tower for a weather forecast. One of the controllers, normally accustomed to a very quiet environment, smiled at me during this turmoil and joked "we're being invaded." Once every year the people of the two communities hold a combined festival with games, food, etc.

The turmoil of the exchange was short-lived; the jetliner departed with a tremendous roar, and then Spitsbergen returned to its quiet isolation. I took long walks in this mountainous country, up over the glaciers and down to the sea. On open expanses there lay fields of mountain poppies (*Papaver nudicaule*) with their pale-yellow, small calices. Some grasses also grow on the clay and rocky slopes, but there is no extensive tundra as such. The island is essentially a glacier-covered desert, just as are the islands of the Canadian Archipelago in similar latitudes. There are a few retreats on the island: Ny Ålesund on Kongsfjorden, and Sveagruva, which are former coalmines. And remarkably, as though living this outpost-life in Longyearbyen were not enough, many of the inhabitants own cabins in "the interior," which are frequented in the way that the people of Minneapolis retreat to their lake cabins in northern Minnesota. But ultimately I needed to solve the problem of the non-functioning starter motor.

I found a good and helpful friend in the Engineer Olav Bergholz. Normally working in Oslo, Bergholz is a resourceful man with flaming red hair who was doing a stint of maintenance work in Spitsbergen on various runway fixtures. The problem that I faced was the absence of any mechanic, and of any parts suitable for light aircraft on Spitsbergen. There were, however, several well-equipped helicopter mechanics. The great service done to me by Olav Bergholz was in providing me with various options. He determined the means of obtaining a replacement starter-motor from Oslo, which could be placed on the next flight from Tromsø a week later. He also determined that one of the local helicopter mechanics had a past experience in light plane maintenance. And this mechanic, working after hours, took on the job of repairing my starter. His biggest job in this, under normal circumstances, trivial piece of repair work, was to machine a new shear pin.

I finally installed the repaired starter-motor, and prepared to depart. My destination Tromsø, although nearly ten degrees of latitude to the south, was still far above the Arctic Circle. I could therefore count on virtually 24 hours of sunlight. But because of the warm tendrils of the Northeast Atlantic Current, an extension of the Gulf Stream, that flow around the north of Norway and into the Barents Sea, I was now leaving the settled arctic weather and flying towards the region of the polar front. Satellite images showed the Barents and Norwegian Seas to be cloud-covered. But these images, combined with earth-bound weather observations, suggested no severe frontal activity, and that I would be dealing simply with horizontal layers of cloud. There was however a strong off-shore wind near Tromsø. This generates severe turbulence along the rugged mountain coast of Norway, and the meteorologist tried to dissuade me from flying there. In addition to this, I would be bucking a 30-knot headwind in crossing the sea. Well, I had flown over windy mountains before. And I had to admit that the heavy rolling and yawing motion at altitudes over mountains in strong winds was quite unpleasant, and I would not subject a passenger to it knowingly. Still, the strength of the wind was not more than I thought I could handle. And the fact that it would take me five hours to cross the sea in the teeth of a headwind— well, I was specially equipped for long-distance flight and marine survival, and I had come to particularly enjoy long flights. Besides, the present conditions had existed for nearly two days, and gave no indication of changing in the near future. In a moment of decisiveness, I chose to depart for the northcape of Norway.

I refiled the flight plan from two days earlier, changing only the date and time of departure. This time the engine started with an eagerness I had not sensed before on this trip. I taxied onto the runway, and the familiar jargon of traffic-directing sounded again in my headset: "November-one-six-four-one-hotel, clear for takeoff." I lifted off to the west with the sun behind me, and gained again that wonderful bird's eye overview as the distant land rose slowly over the limited horizon of the earth-bound observer. It was a wonderful morning! The snowfields and glaciers radiated a pure white among the many rugged peaks and ridges of powder blue-gray rock. The air over Spitsbergen was perfectly clear with azure sky overhead and some lines of white cloud far out over the Greenland Sea. The water expanse of Isfjorden sparkled cold and fresh and blue in this "new beginning." It was to my soul as though air and land and water pollution were distant errors, far removed from this moment and this place. The world was pristine and the air pleasantly cool. And the dazzling star that is the sun circles the blue sky, shepherding this Arctic domain as a sanctuary from the mistakes of civilization.

More by default than by conscious design, I followed the south-shore of Isfjorden overwater to the headland of Kapp

Linné on the opening to the Greenland Sea. The long buildings of Barentsburg stood some miles beyond the entrance of a small side-fjord before that cape. And towards the northwest, I now had another perspective of the ridge of Prins Karls Forland, shining as brightly as when I first saw it five days earlier. I rounded the cape with naught but blue sea to the west. I followed the coastline first south and later south-southeast. This southern portion of Spitsbergen is in the shape of an arrowhead pointing to the distant extreme northern shores of old Europe.

A large indentation in the coast branches off into two broad and long fjords that cut two-thirds (about 40 miles) of the distance across the island here. Parallel to the coast and some 15 miles inland, there is a long and narrow mountain ridge, exposed rock cutting through glacier which is not about to be interrupted and subdued by such a trifle as two majestic fjords crossing it at right angles. Both Van Mijenfjorden and Van Keulenfjorden find their entrance gated by islands lying across their openings. The narrow ridge of Akseløya stands like a fence across the broad opening of the first. Thirty miles farther on a spectacular ice-field (Torellbreen), many miles in length and breadth, slopes down and out into the sea. Then, a final fjord before the very tip of the arrowhead, whose cutting edge of the eastern side is of ice.

As the last of the land passed beneath, the open sea ahead lay veiled in a low cover of sheepskin-textured clouds. To the east, the Barents Sea was clear, and its swells shimmered in the low sunshine over a wide area. To the west, the Norwegian Sea ran a cold clear blue, but also gave off tendrils of sea-smoke which would soon become fog. The Loran navigator decided to stop its antics of flashing skywave warnings and settled down to steady operation. I looked over my shoulder at the beautiful lines of alpine peaks arising from the sea; farewell to Spitsbergen!

Leaving the land behind, barren and rugged though it was, triggered feelings of uneasiness. After all, I was relying on that single engine up front. But somehow that extensive woolly cloud-layer below removed all anxiety by very effectively hiding its source— the cold and high-running sea. Although it gave a soothing feeling to see the soft white below, I would not be fooled. I tried to calculate the length of gliding time between breaking out below the clouds and making contact with the waves. That time may well have been zero because of the high probability of fog over the sea. I therefore called Bjørnøya (Bear Island) which is a single small peak breaking the sea-surface about one third of the way across. Bjørnøya reported a thousand foot ceiling, but their four-kilometer visibility was not wholly reassuring. Well, after planning one's actions for this remote contingency of engine failure, there is not much point in dwelling on it, and I settled down to enjoy the flight and to navigate, occasionally making a change of a few degrees in my heading as the Loran indicated a slow drifting to one side of course or the other. I ate my sandwich, which was a large crescent-shaped roll of fresh bread covered with poppy seeds and filled with slices of cucumber, tomato and Swiss cheese. It tasted delicious— "you may take my word for it," as Nansen might have said of the food they cooked on their journey almost a hundred years earlier. There were only a few items of food to be had in the small shop in Longyearbyen, but what they had was fresh, and suited my palate like a treat. I must say that the fare I encountered from Spitsbergen all the way to Greenland was a very welcome surprise, as I'd given no real thought to food beforehand.

I crossed Bjørnøya in 74°30' N latitude, watching the ADF needle make the slow half-circle transition from pointing straight up to straight down, as I passed by the station. The cloud layer remained perfectly closed and horizontal, far below, and I saw nothing of the small peak. Then a second cloud layer began to form above. At first it was only long and thin rows of condensed vapor, tinted orange and lilac, and crossing obliquely the blue sky beyond. The blue spaces began to fill farther on, and in some directions the space in this developing cloud sandwich began to appear quite dark. The latitude readout of the Loran continued slowly to decrease, and I could tell from the ground-speed readout that I was indeed flying into a headwind.

After several hours of flight between the layers, the undercast began to break up. Between the remaining rows of cloud I then saw a dark sea, heavily agitated, with the crests of the swells blowing off white sheets of spray. Then rifts appeared in the overcast as well, and the blue sky and sunshine emerged once again. But instead of the cloud layers, diffuse cumulus structures with obscured bases stood in the offing.

The foaming surface of the sea was a ragged patchwork of dark and light. The dominating dark areas showed that more than half of the sky was of these convective clouds. The light areas of the sea were of many colors, but dominated by a golden-orange sheen. And here the airplane began to roll and pitch slightly after hours of perfectly smooth sailing. I looked at the estimated time to Tromsø on the Loran readout and found that this estimated time, which had been decreasing, albeit slowly, had now increased. The headwind was picking up.

I tried to peer around the diffuse bulges of the dominating cumuli to see if I could catch a glimpse of the Norwegian coast. But the air was now too misty to see that coast which was still some 50 miles away. In fact the distant atmosphere was somewhat dark, although not threateningly so. I therefore contented myself with the colorful and mottled scenery closer to hand. The only uncomfortable thing about it was that the level of turbulence continued to increase. My altitude began to vary substantially, both up and down by a thousand feet, and I became convinced that I was traversing a regular "mountain wave." This was all becoming a bit too much; I disengaged the autopilot— I should probably have done that a while earlier— and started to hand-fly this bucking machine.

After a short while the mistiness receded a bit, and before me lay some of the fairest scenery I had ever seen. Pale-green mountains rose straight out of the sea to form steep pyramids. Hundreds of these of all sizes stood along a front from the blue-gray misty distances both to the left and right, and they continued on inland. The coastline was heavily invaginated, with long fjords and sounds twisting and curving far inland.

My work was now cut out for me. The airplane was rolling heavily, and it seemed to be punched by sharp blows. This is the price to be paid for this spectacular scenery. I slowed the airplane a bit, to its turbulent air penetration speed. Somewhere deep down among this chaos of mountain ridges with twisting waterfilled valleys was an airport, Tromsø. To find it I needed to rely on VHF navigation because the coastline and the terrain were simply too chaotic to be useful for orientation. I tried to look at the local charts to find the beacon frequencies. But I found it very difficult to pinpoint the numbers as the chart in my hand was jerking about in the blows of the turbulence. Once I'd found the numbers, it was no less difficult to switch them into the radios; effects of the turbulence kept jerking my hand and I switched through the pertinent numbers on the dials. It was no easier to set the volume control to a reasonable level. But even random motion will ultimately land on the desired spot, and finally I reached the desired settings.

The view was truly marvelous. The near mountain heights arose in steep flanks from the valleys far below. This complex perspective was in continuous motion, shifting new mountain walls and new waterways and fjords into view, as others vanished or turned a new aspect to the eye. The sheets of water mirrored the dark green of the high walls flanking the valleys. Many of the high mountain faces were of a gray-green tundra-like vegetation, tilted alpine meadows. But bare rock walls of silver gray streaked with brown exposed layers also jutted forth in this shifting, three-dimensional world in extreme relief. The terrain's aspect shifted smoothly; the nearer structures faster and those in the distance more slowly. Depth perception was strong because of this relative motion. The terrain, of course, simply stood there, unmoved by the turmoil it generated in the air flowing over and around it.

I called the tower to give my approximate distance and direction from the airport, of which I had not seen the slightest sign. I told the tower controller that "the scenery is spectacular." "That's why we live here" was his response. I had switched into my radios the frequencies of a beacon near the airport, and also of the runway localizer. The instrument displays of these were intermittently flagged because of signal blockage due to an intervening outcropping or other. The mountains also distorted the signals; the course needle would move from one side of the gauge to the other, and back again in a random and rapid fashion. The Loran was entirely useless, and I had turned it off long ago. But where was the airport? I knew only that I was bounding in its general direction and that as I neared it the localizer needle, at any rate, would settle down and direct me to the runway threshold. My main task of the moment was to judge mountain heights so as to avoid crashing into one of them, and to maintain my general direction of flight.

As valley after winding valley appeared before me, I finally saw the geometrically straight, light gray runway next and parallel to a long hill ridge on a small green island surrounded by water channels far ahead and far below. A long, curving bridge of flowing lines crossed the channel to the island from the west. An SAS jetliner was about to turn onto final approach ahead of me. Because I had that white needleshaped airplane in sight about ten miles ahead, the tower approved a straight-in approach behind the jet-transport. The tower operator was unwilling (unable, actually) to commit himself to give me the local winds. He recommended caution, and offered only the information that the two windsocks located near the two ends of the runway were pointing at each other, and therefore in opposite directions.

I crossed over a final rocky outcropping that reached out from the mountain height above me to the right, established a crosswind correction to the left because I found myself drifting to the right, and neared the runway threshold, still bouncing, but in considerably less turbulence now in the depths of this valley. The wind died completely over the threshold, and I made an easy landing in the far north of Scandinavia.

During the following week I flew the length of the Norwegian coast, first to Trondheim and finally to Bergen. One can say that Tromsø and Trondheim lie both inland and on the coast simultaneously. Such is the natural topography of Norway. Particularly in the north, but in reality everywhere, the almost innumerable fjords and sounds nearly divide Norway into small pieces. And it certainly boasts a vast number of islands. To the south of Tromsø, but still well to the north of the Arctic Circle, a double-layer of islands overhangs the general trend of the outer coast like eaves, the Vesterålen and Lofoten. And in early August the steep pyramid mountains that constitute these islands radiate with an emerald green. In this regard, their aspect is typical of the hundreds of mountain flanks that face the sea.

These sea-facing flanks are simply the outer reaches of long ridges of mountains that separate the fjords. During the ice age all of Scandinavia was the pedestal of an ice sheet that extended well beyond the present coastline, like an open umbrella, out into the sea. What is now the Baltic Sea was at the center of this ice sheet, much as Hudson Bay was at a similar center on North America. As the earth warmed on the time scale of millenia, the ice sheet retreated, and for a time long fingers of fast moving glaciers ground away the valleys of the fjords. Today, the remaining glaciers lay only on the higher central backbone of the Scandinavian peninsula, and there only in isolated patches. These are surrounded by large expanses of alpine tundra. Even as far south as the vicinity of Bergen, when I was traveling by car through pine forests on this up and down terrain, I would often be surprised by suddenly finding myself on a treeless expanse of tundra vegetation.

But there are many forests in Norway, despite its high latitudes, which correspond to those of Alaska. As in Alaska, these forests owe their existence to the maritime climate, here engendered by the warm Northeast Atlantic Current, which also brings much rain to the mountains. The moist marine air of a westerly wind is forced to rise on the mountain slopes, there to cool and to purge itself of its water. During my flights along this coast I remained out over the water for the greater part of the time. I chose clear days so as to make the most of the scenery. Almost invariably, however, a broken layer of mildly convective cumulus clouds lay over the emerald green pyramids on my left, as I was sailing under a clear blue sky. On the land, rainshowers may be expected at any time.

I stayed three days at Tromsø, at the very pleasant and spacious Scandic Hotel. The hotel stands on the forested hillside overlooking the airport runway in the near distance. Beyond the runway lies the water channel that forms the western boundary of the island, and on which sea birds were nesting among the reeds. Jagged mountain ridges rise on the far side of the channel to form a barrier before the open ocean. But the barrier is interrupted by a deep cleft that forms a water channel connection to the sea outside. The town of Tromsø lies on the other side of the hill ridge behind the hotel on the eastern shore of this small island. And beyond the channel there, the view from the town is of an alpine mountainscape. It is a wonderful combination, this land of mountains and of the sea simultaneously; fields of mountain flowers juxtaposed with quays and fishing boats and harbor structures designed to accommodate the ebb and flow of the tides. The world's northernmost university is in Tromsø.

During my stay in Tromsø I finally undertook the task of rearranging the baggage compartment of the airplane. I'd planned to do this since the start, at which time the rule I followed was simply to load everything on board. I now emptied the entire contents of the baggage compartment onto the tarmac, and then carefully repacked the items. The result was a packed array of bags and cases of the same unruly aspect as the original. After this experience, I made no further attempts at organizing.

After three days the weather had improved sufficiently for a flight to Trondheim, but not to Bergen, which reported low ceilings in continuous rain. I took off with large diffuse pillows of cloud overhead. After some maneuvering because of airline traffic in this narrow valley, I continued to climb among the huge clouds to reach a safe altitude above the local peaks. The sun was dazzlingly reflected from the churning white streamers of the cloudscape, as I headed southwest towards the sea. Passing the last of the pillows, I saw the green chain of mountains of the Lofoten stretching far onward in my direction of flight. The flanks of the mountains are often so steep that sheer cliffs fall into the sea. But the channels are so shallow that boulders dislodged from the cliffs form real hazards to ship-navigation, and I could see the agitated white foam of the water washing over them in the dark shadows of the mountains. The contrast between bright and dark was quite remarkable. The pillows of cloud over the coast were particularly dazzling, and the sun-exposed flanks of the emerald mountains were bright in contrast to the dark green, almost black, mountain flanks in the shade of the clouds, or those facing away from the sun.

I followed the line of Lofoten some distance out to sea, but then decided to angle in toward the coast. I crossed over the airbase at Bodø and ultimately turned inland toward the Trondheim airport, flying over undulating and somewhat less rugged terrain. Long tongues of water continued to pass beneath until I finally saw the head of the fjord beyond which the airport is situated. A hill ridge obstructs the view of the airport from the north until one is quite near, and on this day the sky beyond was dark with rainclouds.

The Germans built the airport, I was told by several people. The main runway has since been extended out over the waters of the bay to accommodate jet transports. It started as a grass strip made level by sport-pilots in the earliest days of aviation and has evolved to become a major airport. A healthy saltwater marsh lives on the shore here, and farther inland I saw cultivated fields in this northern country. The city of Trondheim is many miles from the airport. A pleasant harbor town of stone buildings, Trondheim is an ancient city that was once the capital of a Viking kingdom ruled by King Olav Tryggvason, who founded Trondhjem in 997 A.D.

Back in the control tower I had the good fortune of the offer of a piece of delicious cake with coffee. It was the birthday of one of the controllers.

From Trondheim I flew due west for a good while, following the broad fjord there before turning south around the town of Ålesund to follow the immensely complex coastline of skerries down to Bergen. In Norway it's perfectly acceptable to file a VFR flight plan with the route listed as "coastwise." As everywhere else in Europe and in most other parts of the world the air traffic controllers will respond in English to an English-speaking pilot. But they will respond in the local language if the pilot communicates in that language. On a later occasion at Reykjavik I was awaiting a clear space on the frequency to request clearance to cross a runway. I was a long time awaiting such an opening in a flood of radio exchanges in Icelandic.

I arrived at Flesland-Bergen airport under a variable low ceiling with scattered rainshowers, after having made room— for the third time in Norway— for an SAS jetliner with landing priority. I followed my usual procedure of obtaining a daily weather briefing, normally by visiting the meteorological offices in person. The remainder of the days afforded excellent opportunities to explore the environs and to sample the cuisine. This was especially pleasant because of my fondness for fish and seafood, and good firm bread and flavorful coffee. I found mackerel and herring particularly delightful for breakfast.

Bergen is an old Hanseatic town with a population proud of its cultural history. The old buildings of earlier capitalist trade provide the waterfront with a pleasing scenery. Because the weather over the Atlantic was slow to improve, I took the welcome opportunity to drive far and wide inland along the many fjords and over the mountains. The number of road tunnels is quite remarkable. But often the road leads over or along a mountain ridge. And there one emerges from a pine forest onto sparse alpine meadows containing lakes with rocky shores. At other times one climbs through terraced valleys of all shades of luminous green with glaciers shining from the heights in the distance, and waterfalls spilling over palisades.

Norwegian coast to the north of the Arctic Circle.

Volcano on the west coast of Iceland, north of Reykjavik.

Chapter 6

OCEAN FLIGHT ALONG THE ARCTIC CIRCLE

Land and sea, equatorial and polar; these pairs form complex "duals" for generating weather and determining climates on the surface of the planet. Land has a relatively low capacity for heat, and therefore changes its temperature rapidly with changes in solar illumination; the surface temperature of a landmass fluctuates substantially between day and night. The sea, on the other hand, tends to remain near its seasonal average temperature, fluctuating little during the 24 hours. Because of its slow response, the temperature of the ocean also varies much less throughout the year than that of a continent in mid and high latitudes.

Moderating the temperature fluctuations, like the coolant of a car engine, is the atmospheric air, which is set in motion by the very temperature gradients that it will thereby reduce. Over land the surface air is heated by the warming ground, and begins to rise in mid-morning. It carries off some of the surface heat. By early afternoon the rising thermals may reach an altitude at which the air can no longer contain its water vapor and clouds begin to form. The condensation of the vapor into liquid cloud-droplets releases heat into the air. And if the moisture content is high, the condensation acts like a continuous burner on a hot air balloon; it boosts the thermals to rise ever higher, thus forming the well-known isolated thunderstorms of summer. At Iqaluit I later saw a wonderful satellite photo showing the domed cloud tops obscuring totally the land surface of a section of Baffin Island. Over the neighboring Labrador Sea and Davis Strait the air was perfectly clear, exposing the dark surface of the water. It was actually possible to trace the coastline, including bays and narrow fjords, by simply following the edge of the afternoon cloud cover on the satellite image.

Land can also harbor immense volumes of ice, glaciers that are hundreds of thousands of years old. Sea ice, on the other hand, is rarely more than ten years old. Of course, thermals will never form over an ice sheet. And great landmasses also confine and therefore direct the courses of ocean currents.

These great currents of the fluid sea are set in motion by great patterns of wind, patterns on a scale as large as the distances between polar and equatorial regions. The tropical and subtropical regions receive vertical sunlight, and therefore a large flux of energy. In the arctic regions, sunlight is oblique or nonexistent. Without the atmosphere there would be far greater differences in temperature between the arctic and the tropics than there really are, as it is on the airless moon between the lunar day and night. But on the earth the temperature differences generate great convection patterns which force the warm tropical air north and the cold polar air south. And these winds set the surface of the sea in motion with warm convection currents flowing north and cold currents flowing south.

The Arctic Circle defines the extreme boundary of those lands and seas onto which the oblique midnight sun, shining over the North Pole, casts its rays at least briefly at the summer-solstice. This boundary curve crosses over much land, but over only one long stretch of open water across the North Atlantic Ocean. It lies on the sea at only four other locations, for short distances, across Davis Strait, Foxe Basin, Bering Strait and the inland White Sea of the Soviet

Union. And over the North Atlantic, the circle itself is crossed by two powerful and opposing ocean currents.

Flowing south across the Arctic Circle through Denmark Strait to the east of Greenland is a large stream of cold water from the Arctic Ocean, its sea-ice melting during the passage. Checked in its southward flow by the even mightier Gulf Stream, the East Greenland Current turns around Cape Farewell at the southern tip of Greenland to flow northward along its western coast toward Davis Strait. An eddying branch of the current continues south along the North American coast as the Labrador Current. This is ultimately swirled away by the powerful warm waters that arise in the basins of the Caribbean Sea and the Gulf of Mexico.

The warm Gulf Stream, overlain by air that is nearly saturated with water vapor in the temperate latitudes, crosses the ocean to the east. A warm extension of the Gulf Stream, the Northeast Atlantic Current touches the shores of Iceland. And when the winds have a southerly component and are forced upward over the volcanic mountains, the air cools adiabatically and creates massive and ice-laden clouds, especially in mid-summer. Farther east, the contact between the arctic air and the air over the Northeast Atlantic Current can lead to widespread condensation into extensive layers of stratus clouds. Pilots are generally not greatly disturbed by the opaqueness of clouds; we simply fly by reference to the flight instruments. It is the indirect effects of icing (ice-buildup on the airframe and propeller, or at the air intake of the engine) and turbulence that make us wary. And clouds with these potentials we try to avoid.

I was about to set out along an established ferry route across the North Atlantic, a couple of degrees south of the Arctic Circle. Even though established, it is nonetheless notorious for its icing potential. I had spent some days in

Norway, making my way slowly south along her coast, at ease, all the while watching the weather slowly improve as a ridge of high pressure was building over the Norwegian mountains. And now, in Bergen, this high pressure was becoming a curse. Welcome though it was while coasting along Norwegian fjords, it presented a problem farther out to sea. A weather front lay over the ocean and the Færöe Islands, curving from southwest to north-northeast some 500 miles off the Norwegian coast. I looked at the North Atlantic weather charts daily— after all, it's important to form a picture of the atmospheric dynamics, and this takes time— but the front remained stationary. That in itself presented no serious problem; I knew that it would be nearly impossible to avoid at least one front in crossing this ocean. Troubling was an unending string of storms tracking northward along that front. The atmospheric pressure ridge over the land was called a "blocking high" because it deflected all attempts of these low-pressure systems from penetrating to the land. This was good for the Norwegians because it gave them beautiful summer weather, with the storms remaining at sea. But for me it finally became a question of timing; I would have to time my takeoff propitiously so as to slip through in the space between two storms.

Thus I took off from Flesland airport and turned to the west. The airplane was slightly overgross in weight, with full wing tanks and about 45 gallons in the cabin tank. This gave me a range of nearly 2000 miles. But the weight demanded vigilance in crossing a coastal ridge between the airport and the shoreline outside. Low mountain ridges with many points stood in all directions, separating valleys filled with water channels of complicated and intricate shorelines. Some low clouds were hanging over the complex relief topography. The airport itself, now to my left-rear, is in a relatively broad depression of this wild natural scenery.

The coastal ridge was treeless. Though not high, it had the character of an alpine meadow with weather-stunted grasses on an uneven rocky surface, and large boulders strewn here and there. And beyond lay the unending expanse of the Atlantic Ocean with the sun smiling on its surface swells. The coastline is dotted with many small islets, just offshore. They were low and flat; bright green in color, and surrounded by black submerged rocks that were washed by the soapy foam of the breakers, sloshing back and forth. Farther out over the sea there were patchy areas of low altocumulus clouds.

It seemed remarkable that I could plan and even envision a long flight over open ocean, have adequate reserves of fuel, confidence in the engine, and ready responses to virtually any contingency. And yet, when face to face with the reality of a receding coastline behind, I felt ambivalent and hesitant. No matter how realistically I tried to imagine the flight beforehand, I felt daunted by the sheer vastness of the unending expanse of water before me. It felt as though I were, quite literally, facing infinity. I nevertheless continued on, if only because that saved me the trouble of turning the airplane. In reality, of course, there was never any doubt about continuing. Ahead lay an alluring adventure; the realization of a childhood dream. And all of the mundane, technical aspects of flight were unfolding just as expected.

The feelings of hesitation were quite transitory. By the time I had the Loran receiver on line and was tracking a course to the first waypoint, my spirit was as one with this beautiful water-planet. Floating over the blue rippling expanse were woolly clouds at all distances from directly below to the far away horizon. The ocean reflected a muted metallic glint in the direction of the sun; the subtle movement of distant swells gave a dynamic to its visual texture. After leaving the coast, Bergen local control handed me over to Stavanger oceanic control. Being on a visual flight plan at 5500 feet of altitude I was not required to maintain radio contact. Even so, I followed instrument flight rules (IFR) as closely as possible, maintaining radio contact and giving position reports on a series of radio frequencies, as they were given to me by a string of controllers. It seemed only natural to do so. In any sudden emergency I could then simply key the microphone and transmit my precise position to an operator already aware of my presence, without first hunting for someone to respond on the international emergency frequency.

About 45 minutes into the flight, Stavanger suddenly turned me over to Shetland control. This sounded suspicious to me because my route lay to the north of Scottish or Shetland oceanic airspace. According to the chart, I should be avoiding the northeastern corner of that airspace by some 12 nautical miles, and should instead by approaching north-Atlantic airspace in Reykjavik's jurisdiction. I nevertheless switched to the Shetland frequency and asked them if their radar showed me to be so far off course. No, I was precisely on course— the credit goes to the Loran navigator— but that course took me directly over a North Sea oil platform. And on that course I was in potential conflict with a helicopter awaiting clearance for takeoff. I looked straight down, but for the moment a cloud layer with few openings obscured the surface, and I could see no platform structures. A few seconds later, there it was, through an irregular opening in the undercast, a giant square spider of long legs, standing on the sea. And some distance away there stood another.

But Shetland was the wrong controller after all. They finally asked me to contact "Viking Control" on yet another frequency, in order to coordinate my flight with that of the helicopter.

After this flurry of radio-chatter, the world became quiet and peaceful again. The far edge of the undercast drew nearer and then fell behind. And there lay the ocean, leaden and heavy in its miniature surface movements, the rolling swells rising and falling but always drawn back powerfully to their mean sea level. It seemed a wonder to me that this unending water surface should be able to find its level everywhere; and everywhere be able to follow the minute curvature of the enormous spherical surface of the earth. And all attempts of the sea to free itself from this constrained shape amount to nothing more than minute wiggles, microscopic fluctuations of rebellion that are everywhere and continually crushed. But the fluctuations and their dynamics are enough to give the surface a visual texture that is essentially different from that of a polished steel sphere, which, I suppose, it would otherwise resemble.

For some time I had been watching long streamers of distant clouds emerging from the horizon ahead and extending south. As time drew on, these rose higher in the sky, and their southern extremities moved farther to my left until their pointed tips were abeam of the airplane. A thin but opaque layer of puffy clouds began to form far below, a few hundred feet over the sea. Behind and to my right, the sky was a peaceful blue.

The northern extremity of the high clouds was emerging from a point on the horizon that lay slightly to the right of the nose of the airplane. It almost seemed as though I could avoid the weather by changing my course just a nudge to the right. But this I knew to be an illusion; if I were to follow this fancy of remaining clear of the weather, I would be forced to continue turning to the right, by small degrees, until at last I would be flying north-northeast and parallel to the Norwegian coast. No, this front must be penetrated.

When approaching weather that appears on the horizon, the clouds rise very slowly at first. But once some portion of cloud has moved abeam of the airplane, things begin to change rapidly. I looked around at the blue sky to the right and behind, but the knife-edge of a torn sheet of stratus was already slicing the air a few hundred feet below. Then another, a couple of hundred feet above. What had earlier been long streamers across the sky quickly became a dark gray and imposing overcast. The torn stratus sheets began to fill and quickly became continuous layers. I found myself flying in a drab-gray sandwich whose cloud slices were rapidly thickening. Behind I could still see a horizontal strip of blue, but as I looked back, the shifting perspective of the cloud layers suddenly swallowed it up.

Off to my left the lower stratus slice began to dip away, and I saw the domes of luminous greenish cumulus structures faintly outlined against the dark overcast clouds. Then suddenly the stratus layer just below tilted upwards and the outside world was closed off. Dense and uniform gray was the world on the other side of the windows; all sense of up or down was gone, as was all sense of distance or movement. Small rivulets of water streamed over the surface of the wings, up over the windshield, and horizontally along the side windows, whipping off a shower of droplets from all trailing edges of the airplane. With nothing else to see on the outside, I began a slow scan of the cockpit instruments. The outside air temperature was about 12° C, well above freezing. All systems were functioning normally, yet a daunting feeling came over me.

The feeling was in consequence of mental reflections—thinking— about my present situation in this world. There is nothing daunting about instrument flight as such. But here I was hurtling through opaque air 5000 feet over an ocean, hundreds of miles from any land. I felt it my duty to reflect on the proper responses to sudden engine failure. And this conjures up images of the airplane awash on the surface of the sea in a heavy squall. At least there was no danger of slamming into a hillside, or a tree, or a concrete wall during the descent.

But the ocean swells present their own forms of treachery. The "rules" state that a water-landing is to be carried out in the direction parallel to the major waves. But the sudden contact with the water surface can flip the airplane upside down, or cause it to cartwheel if a wingtip strikes a wave. I suppose that many pilots carry with them the images of a pushed-out windshield, the result of striking it with their forehead during the sudden deceleration. And then one imagines oneself struggling into the survival suit, making sure to have the hand-held ELT (emergency locator transmitter) inside the suit. That done, and standing on the submerged and slippery wing, one pulls out the heavy pack that contains the life raft; to inflate it. And all of this must be carried out while the airplane is rolling heavily in an eight-foot swell.

After reviewing all of this carefully, and also the various initial steps of transmitting the predicament and precise position, and of all the details that might be the cause of an engine failure in the first place so that I could make a systematic restart attempt, I settled down once more to actually enjoy this flight. I was in fact in a somewhat euphoric state, which I think is shared by most pilots flying small, single-engine aircraft across an ocean. Two days later, at the Loftlaiðir Hotel on the Reykjavik airport, I met a man who was flying a similar airplane in the opposite direction. He was about to set off for the Færöe Islands and seemed incapable of containing his ebullient joy. His face absolutely beamed. And there was a spring in his stride such as I had rarely seen before.

I had been flying in undifferentiated soup for about 45 minutes when I began to see subtle shadings in the horizontal layers. The scenery— such as it was— then changed rapidly. An enormous misty cavern appeared to my left; the sensation came over me that the airplane would tip over and slide down into this deep gray hole. On the other side of it stood the cauliflower heads of cumulus clouds. These heads were not in the clear, but stood in the dark shade of the deep and undifferentiated cloud overhead and on all sides. A person just leaving home and looking at the weather, would call the outlook dreary. The cumuliform structures had the visual texture of milkglass with the milkiness of a greenish light gray. Then I was sailing right over the top of more of these cauliflower domes, occasionally clipping a corner. And finally the air began to lighten and I emerged into misty blue sky.

Behind me was a mountain range of cloud, and the vertical wall of that range towered above me and angled off to my right in the one o'clock direction. Just in front, and at the bottom of the steep slope, there lay rugged islands emerging from the ocean. Their steep flanks terminated in broken points and ridges along the crests of the islands, and about half of their surface was enshrouded by fog and clouds. But enough of their wild and rough surface was exposed to view to show an emerald green surface covering. It was undoubtedly of grasses that could drink their fill of dew and rainwater in this watery environment.

From my perspective at 5500 feet, these islands appeared tropical and volcanic because of both the lushness of their green color and their tall and rugged, almost shaft-like aspect. And on the only low and flat corner of one of these islands there was a single, hard-surfaced and well-maintained runway, or so it appeared, at any rate, from my altitude. The air still contained individual large clouds, and the runway emerged from beneath one of these as I sailed on.

I called the radio operator of these Færöe Islands, giving my position and estimated time to "Ten West," my next reporting point on the way to Iceland. As I crossed the radio beacon, I turned 15° to the right for a direct heading to Iceland. The tall frontal clouds on my right were now slowly receding and appeared to curve more and more to the north. The sky was clearing wonderfully ahead, but I couldn't help looking back to the left at the surprisingly beautiful Færöe Islands. I had a strong inclination to land. But my time was growing short and I still had Greenland to cross, as well as several treacherous stretches of icy ocean, and I did not think that I could spare the time.

As the Færöe islands were now receding I saw their tremendous power as local "weather factories." They uplift the humid air on the weather side, generating wonderfully sculpted banks of cloud that curve smoothly around and over the jagged land. Two of the islands were entirely enshrouded, trailing large billows for some distance downwind. It was as though large quantities of steam were issuing forth from the land surface, obliterating it, and the steam was then slowly carried away by the wind until it dissipated far to the lee of the islands.

Ahead, the sky was perfectly clear. And the ocean seemed to extend forever. The sun was now a little ahead of my left wing, and the surface in that direction was of a bronze color. Everywhere the surface was rippling and shimmering with the perturbations in slow dynamic motion, moving in several directions at once. In the far distance toward the sun there was a collection of small, soft and warm-looking cloud puffs low over the sea. They took on golden hues that blended well with the metallic background of the ocean. To the north the ocean was clear and cold blue. And the blue sky reached down to it far away on the horizon.

A half hour after passing the Færöe archipelago the Loran showed that I was approaching "Ten West," a compulsory reporting point when IFR. Ten West is a completely undistinguished location at 62°37'N, 10°00'W. Apart from transmitting this position back to the Færöe Islands radio operator, it served to remind me to switch over from the now nearly empty ferry tank to the fuel in my wing tanks; I had been underway for nearly four hours. And from beyond the horizon ahead there arose a thin and abrasively glaring, rough white line.

This line was evidently composed of cloud, directly illuminated by the sun, but I could only see the very top of it. The bulk of the clouds was hidden from my view by the downward curvature of the earth's surface. They were so far away that even had I seen the whole of them, they would have appeared miniscule. There were none of the outstretching or overhanging purplish streamers that reach high up into the sky from beyond the horizon, as those that had announced the distant frontal weather earlier. They seemed so low that I could easily overfly them without climbing, I thought. The only thing even mildly troubling about them was that they appeared to be so agitated, so active, and so dense. And this, together with their brilliant whiteness, conjured up images of severe turbulence and icing. Could it be that these clouds stood over Iceland itself?

That thought reminded me of the Polynesians and the Vikings. These truest of navigators employed the stars, the winds and the waves, and the color of the ocean and of the atmosphere to shape their sure course across immense distances of open ocean. They, I am certain, would have recognized these cloud-tops beyond the horizon as anchored to land, without the question-mark.

For an hour I observed this band of clouds, rising out of the ocean, as the line of the horizon descended and exposed more and more of the clouds' lower, previously hidden structure. And then I saw a very thin line of low coast, a light metallic gray, lying on the distant blue ocean just before the bases of the clouds. According to the Loran I was then about 60 miles southeast of Iceland, and about to cross the boundary between the Reykjavik oceanic and domestic airspaces. I called the Reykjavik controller to inform him of this, and was given a new radio frequency for my continuing flight within the domestic area.

The new controller acknowledged my radio call, and began immediately to ask my further intentions. He was evidently of the opinion that I would not be able to stay out of the clouds at 5500 feet. And if I were to ascend to 6000 feet or higher to stay clear of the clouds I would need an IFR (instrument) clearance anyway. Some domestic flights over Iceland had given him pilot reports that indicated cloud tops of 8000 to 12,000 feet. The surface winds were blowing from the southeast at 35 knots. There were intermittent rainshowers over Reykjavik and the freezing level was at 6000 feet.

I tried to absorb all of this. And usually, when faced with adverse information I tend to reflect first on the worst piece, and then go on from there.

That wind velocity of 35 knots sounded pretty ominous. But it seemed to be a steady wind, not very gusty, and pretty much aligned with Reykjavik runway 14. A freezing level of 6000 feet wouldn't be a problem if I flew at 5500 feet, which I still thought I might be able to manage without entering the clouds; from my perspective at that point the cloud tops ahead appeared to be just below my altitude. After reaching a radio beacon on the southeast coast of Iceland, my planned course was a straight line from there to another beacon near the airport, some 150 miles due west across southern Iceland. And if the clouds there should prove to be too tall, I could instead fly farther south, along the coast, and avoid these convective cloud masses which were generated by the powerful uplifting of the 35 knot oceanic air by the mountains of Iceland. Thus, my response to the controller was simple: for the moment I would continue on according to the flight plan.

I then crossed the coastline. The land beyond it seemed to be a low washout plain with several meandering streams flowing across it, toward the sea. The coast itself was a barrier sandbar that harbored tidal pools on the side toward the land. Farther inland, everything was obscured by the clouds.

For a short while I remained on top of the overcast. But it soon became clear that I would need to climb to stay out of the clouds. I requested an IFR clearance and an altitude of 8000 feet. The radio operator immediately cleared me to 8000 and turned me over to Keflavik for IFR control on another frequency. Keflavik issued clearance limits and asked me to report reaching 8000. A few moments later he called again to relay a pilot report from a domestic airliner that cloud tops over central Iceland were now up to 18000 feet with moderate icing in the clouds. If I should need to go higher than 8000, the flight levels above me were available, and if I were unable to outclimb the clouds, I should then deviate to the south.

Still climbing toward 8000, an opening appeared to my right. And there I saw a gleaming glacier field spread over a jagged mountain range of dark basalt. A large circular hole in the undercast to the left exposed more of the extensive washout plain on this southeastern coast of Iceland. The clouds below, ahead and to the right were brilliant white and billowing, with sharp and dynamic edges, and obviously building actively. Eight thousand feet wouldn't do; I asked for ten, and later still for 12000 feet, both of which were instantly approved.

Twelve-thousand appeared to be adequate. But Keflavik asked me repeatedly about flight conditions. The energetic domes of the large cumulus clouds skimmed close by below. They were a little higher to my right, as was an occasional one to the left. Streamers and swirls coiled through the air, thus accenting the dynamic motion of these cloud tops. Contour-following sheets of stratus overlay some of the cumulus domes. I was primed to turn south and out over the ocean if any of this should come too near. But the cloudscape to the south was not exactly falling away rapidly. And if I were to choose that option, it would be some time before I'd reach a more comfortable spacing below.

Of course, my other option was to continue to climb. But with minor deviations, both to the left and to the right, I managed substantially to remain in the clear. And then as if out of nowhere, one of the contour-following stratus blankets stretched right across my course from beam to beam. I felt confident that I would be through it in a matter of seconds, but I was in the grip of a curiosity to see just what I would find inside that curving cloud layer. The thermometer showed -10°.

I punched into the cloud and instantly streaks of liquid water washed up over the windshield and the wings. I was fascinated by the phenomenon. Imagine, liquid water with eighteen degrees Fahrenheit of frost; it seemed somehow unnatural. But time was advancing in slow motion; a second or two later the supercooled streaming water rigidified, and formed a thin layer of clear ice over the windshield and the wings.

The seconds were dragging on as though they were minutes, but I broke out of the cloud as suddenly as I had entered it. Through the side windows I saw that the clouds were lower ahead. And then, slowly, the thin layer of ice on the windshield began to sublimate with the help of the propeller blast and the 125 knot wind blowing over it.

As is common when IFR, there was a good deal of radio exchange. After what seemed a long time, I was finally within range of the Keflavik radar. The controller informed me that I would receive radar vectors (that is, directions given by radio according to my radar blip), to the ILS runway 14 approach to Reykjavik, and that my present heading was "good." He again inquired about my flight conditions, and informed me that when I came nearer to the airport, he would give me a rapid descent through the freezing level, so as to minimize the buildup of ice. There was a rainshower moving across the airport at that moment, he said, and that I should be able to see the tall buildup that was producing it, pushing well above the average cloud-tops in my area. And there it stood, to my right-front, a monster both in circumference and height, and slowly evolving outward on all sides. The cloudscape directly ahead was much lower, and I so informed the controller.

"At pilot's discretion, descend to 5000. Report leaving 12000 and 6000," was his response.

"Leaving 12000 for 5. Report passing 6000," I acknowledged, as I began a fairly steep descent.

The towering mountain of cloud was now slowly drifting by on my right, and some minutes later it fell behind. The cloudscape ahead was far below, ragged and torn, and of all shades of white and gray. I reported passing 6000 feet, and through the dark areas of the clouds I now saw rough volcanic land, some of it a patchy luminous green, and intermittent complex shorelines, all drifting far below across the small openings.

"Continue descent, maintain 2000, turn right heading 050 degrees, base leg," was the next instruction.

As I started the turn, I was immediately enveloped by dense clouds. It was dark inside after the brightly lit cloudscape above. I took off my sunglasses, and had just managed to complete the turn when I heard: "Continue descent to 1200; turn further right, heading 130 degrees; final approach ILS runway 14; seven miles from the marker; contact the tower now."

I acknowledged, and thanked the controller— it had been a pleasure to converse with him. As I centered the localizer needle I broke out of the clouds into a misty cavern of air over open water. About two miles ahead there hung a cloud curtain to within a few hundred feet of the sea, eliminating any chance of seeing the airport or its environs. The airport diagram on the approach chart indicated that the approach-end of runway 14 pushes out into the sea on a short artificial peninsula. Thus there would be no visual cues as to the distance to the airport until I saw the approach light structures or the airport itself.

I rechecked the most important items on the landing checklist, continued to scan the instruments and suddenly saw the red-bordered placard that I had taped to the instrument panel just before leaving home: "Reel in HF antenna before landing." For a moment I hesitated. I was near the surface, an unknown but certainly short distance from the runway threshold, with torn rags of wet clouds flitting past my ears. If I left the antenna extended its drag-funnel would be smashed on the concrete surface at touchdown, with a resulting long flexible copper wire dancing uncontrollably about in the high wind near landing gear and spinning propeller. My choices were to execute the "missed approach," or to begin madly to reel in the antenna, which involved about 25 turns of the wheel followed by setting its friction lock. I reeled it in, undoubtedly accompanied by some weaving back and forth along the localizer course; to execute the missed approach for such a reason seemed just to irritating at that point.

My descent took me just under the leading edge of a low cloud, some 250 feet above the sea, and there a half mile ahead was the runway threshold with the entire, sprawling airport behind it. The wind was still at 35 knots, and individual large raindrops were shattering on the windshield as the airplane touched down and rolled out on Reykjavik airport.

I stayed three days in Iceland, awaiting reasonable weather for my overflight of the Greenland icecap. That same strong southeasterly flow that I had had to contend with on landing was also blowing over Greenland. And I could imagine the kind of icing that I would not be able to outclimb, and that was generated when the warm and moist oceanic air was forced up and over the vast, two-mile thick icefield of Greenland.

It suited me to spend some time in Iceland. I took long and soothing swims and baths in hot springs saturated with minerals. One need not be an expert to recognize the recent volcanic origin of the land, with cindercones along the horizon and porous, lichen-covered rocks with abrasive edges strewn about in deep layers over large areas, and steam issuing forth here and there. Traveling by car in other directions I encountered mountainous terrain covered by a rich green carpet of grasses and beautiful, small tundra flowers. I saw crater lakes with new volcanic domes rising in their center, and occasional deep fissures across the land with sheer walls of dark basalt. Sheep wander over the land, individually or in small clusters, with heavy coats of wool reminiscent of lions' manes. And there are well maintained ranches with low and expansive white buildings surrounded by enormous meadows with rows of freshly cut hay. An occasional rider on horseback may drift across the luminous green meadowland, and multiple sheets of low stratus, tinted lavender, may sail in from the open ocean to the south.

The weather was very changeable in Iceland that August. I encountered much drizzly weather, but also clear sky. From a high point on the airport road I once saw the entire city of Reykjavik, its low skyline of buildings and towers emerge from an overcast day into radiant early evening sunlight. It was like a glorious awakening, the houses and spires all sparkling white on the undulating plain at the edge of the sea with mountains across the bay.

I walked to the Meteorological, or MET Building on a hill near the edge of town daily, to look at weather charts and forecasts. In early morning I telephoned to get a general impression of the conditions over Greenland for that day. It seemed that those conditions were invariably worse than forecast on the evening before. Thus I had expected to depart on the third day. But when I called in the morning the forecaster said, "You cannot go today! There are 50 knot winds reported at Kulusuk and Søndrestrømfjord." The winds were still strong, but less so on the day after, and I decided to fly to Greenland.

I filed a flight plan for the route from Reykjavik across Denmark Strait to the Kulusuk radio beacon on the east coast of Greenland, and from there across the icecap direct to Søndrestrømfjord on the west coast. The airplane had already been fueled earlier, with the wing tanks topped off and the ferry tank about half filled. That tank was only partially filled because I somehow knew that I'd be forced to climb to over 13000 feet over Greenland, and I wanted to be under gross weight for that climb. The engine oil had also been changed at Reykjavik.

As I walked to the airplane I noticed that the tire on the nosewheel was flat. It was Saturday and to repair or replace that tire would be an all-day affair. I rolled the plane forward a bit and the tire itself appeared to be in good condition. I theorized that perhaps some supercooled water had frozen in the tire valve on that flight through ice-laden clouds a few days earlier, and that that had caused a slow leak. A fuel truck was nearby, and they could provide compressed air. The tire seemed to hold the pressure well, at least during the short time that I was still on the ground at Reykjavik, and I decided to take off and later to take care to land softly at Søndrestrøm; if it had been one of the main wheel tires I'd have waited a bit longer and been a little more careful.

Thus, I left Iceland and climbed slowly into a world of blue and white; blue water and sky, and white clouds and ice. Only a minute or two after takeoff this world extended into the far distance on all sides. The well-known sea with its slowly rolling grid of blue waves and occasional foaming and spreading whitecaps reached into the misty distance from below. There were large blankets with irregular edges of a low altocumulus layer enshrouding that sea in various directions. As I lifted above that layer, an icecapped volcano stood radiant in the clear air in the middle distance to the right. It was a symbolic sentry of Iceland, the blue— born of distance— along its lower flanks, and capped like Fujisan with a symmetric cone of softly radiating white ice. I was sailing through pristine space, sparkling, clear, sharp and peaceful, out over Denmark Strait toward an unseen shore.

Greenland was three hours away. An hour into the flight I passed the reporting point "XRAY" in 64°38'N, 26°58'W. Soon after I attempted to establish HF radio contact on a frequency given to me earlier while filing the flight plan. This channel turned out to be saturated with radio traffic, all from far away aircraft, and I gave up the attempt. Two hours into the flight brought high streamers of cloud into view, emerging from a point beyond the horizon to the south.

Fjord coast of East Greenland to the north of Kulusuk.

Icebergs on a fjord of Greenland. Bottom: Minutes later, the eastern margin of the Greenland Icecap appeared.

Chapter 7

GREENLAND, DAVIS STRAIT AND HUDSON BAY

The ocean can take on surprising colors and shades, depending on many factors including the form into which atmospheric moisture has condensed into suspended mists and clouds, and particularly on the angle of solar illumination. Since Iceland my world was dominated by azure and white, both above and below. But now I saw a pink patchwork faintly emerging from the mist on the horizon ahead and dissolving in the distance to the north. It took me some few seconds to recognize it as a coastline rather than a line of clouds, so diffuse were its edges; the mist and the distance softened the jagged edges which one might expect to see on a mountainous fjord-coast. But the mist could not fully hide the random patchwork in miniature detail caused by the vertical folds packed with snow, and the differential shading of the mountain flanks as their polygonal faces angle in many directions.

It was not long before the outline of the mountains became distinct, with scattered skerries outside and sounds between, and sharply defined fjords cutting through the valleys between the pointed peaks. Now that I was sure of the coastline it was also evident that the sea to the north was clear of clouds, and that the atmosphere had the visual texture of a dewy morning mist. Everything was so wonderfully pure and wonderfully soft. I rejoiced in the sensation of a wakeful feeling of morning without tension.

The pink hue of the mountain flanks gradually changed into the rich metallic gray color of their rocky substance as

I approached the shore. Now, too, the patchwork of snowfields on their upper flanks stood out in all their pristine purity. Huge blocks of ice of fantastic shapes lay drifting on the surface of the sea. They shone with a brilliant white with some vertical faces of a luminous pure green. To the south there was a low layer of clouds over the sea with mist above and high clouds streaming out of a somewhat darker atmosphere and curving northward.

I was crossing the boundary between Reykjavik Oceanic Control and the Søndrestrøm Flight Information Region when the Loran threw up its hands in electronic frustration, and in its technical jargon said as much as "I give up, I can't get any decent signals around here anywhere." Well, it was nice while it lasted, and the failure wasn't unexpected. But now it was a question of getting back to basic flying. For a short while I would still be tracking the Kulusuk NDB— my ADF receiver had already acquired the Kulusuk signal— but then it would be back to good old-fashioned dead reckoning over an extensive ice-mass without identifiable surface features.

The strip of land before the glacier was a bare desert. The small islands in front were low and rounded; one of these harbored the Kulusuk runway. But the fjord-coast beyond the skerries pierced the water surface and rose pointing to the sky in triangular fashion, more steeply than pyramids. At 7000 feet, the peaks ahead were well above my altitude of 5500, and between the peaks I could already see the edge of the great dome of ice beyond, a dome that would force me to at least double, and more likely triple my altitude, in order to cross it. For a distance of 350 miles I would be overflying an enormous mass of glacier ice, about 10,000 feet thick, its surface curving in the form of a shield that covers nearly the entire island of Greenland. This glacier is second in mass and extent only to the antarctic ice cap, and in our present geological era has no other rival on earth. The extended ice blanket of the Agassiz Ice Cap on Ellesmere Island, for example, is a mere film of ice by comparison.

One can well imagine that the profound cooling effect of such a body of ice on a moist oceanic air mass flowing from southeast to northwest will generate clouds with a great capacity for icing. Lifting first over the mountain barrier along the Greenland coast, and then over the gentle upslope of the glacier shield, the air will purge itself of its moisture which is then suspended in clouds of small supercooled water droplets. Depending on their size, these droplets will lead to a rapid and debilitating buildup of either rime or clear ice on any hapless aircraft unable to clear the cloud layers. I had already had a small taste of this icing potential over Iceland. And, unfortunately, there was a strong southeasterly flow as I approached the coast.

With the airplane configured and trimmed for cruise-climb, I was looking straight down at the island of Kulusuk, barren and peaceful in the sunshine. There, also, was the runway, a long straight strip of a lighter shade of the same tan color as its surroundings. I called Kulusuk on VHF, telling them that I was crossing the Kulusuk NDB on a VFR flight plan to Søndrestrømfjord. To the north I could see the surfaces of three fjords, densely covered with icebergs opening onto Denmark Strait, one behind the other, with jagged mountain ridges between them. The nearest fjord was of a dark blue color, flanked abruptly by a steep mountain wall. The farther two were of successively lighter shades of blue. Torn sheets of snowfields lay spread on the upper flanks of the mountain ridges. Directly ahead was the crest of a sharply pointed mountain, and behind it a broad and branching fjord cut deeply into the land in a northerly direction. The branches all terminated in massive glacier walls, of whose substance a myriad of icebergs of all sizes lay adrift on the blue waters. To the south was a complex landscape of rocky valleys and steep mountains.

By this time I was at 9000 feet and maintaining a shallow climb. The outside air temperature had already dropped to - 9° C and was slowly decreasing. Cascading down onto the last rocky slopes was the edge of the Greenland ice cap. The ice edge was a steep and vertically somewhat furrowed slope of 1000 feet, and even more in the gaps between the mountain-rock wall. It was of a generally light gray shade, and near its top it began, first slowly, and then in a more determined fashion to curve over and merge with the upper surface of the shield, which was pure white.

I had dreamed of overflying this enormous glacier in clear weather, anticipating a flight of several hours over a pristine, featureless field of white. But ahead was a pastel maroon-colored, diffuse bank of fog, and transparent sheets and filaments of stratus of the same hue were already passing barely 100 feet below the wings. The color was produced by the dimming effects of higher rows of altocumulus clouds and the shading of the ice surface by the stratus sheets themselves. It was now a question of remaining clear of all condensed moisture, because the ice contained in this might quickly overwhelm the airplane.

I gauged my chances of climbing over the soft-edged cloud layer ahead by maintaining the present course and climb configuration, and tentatively concluded that I would remain clear. But a glacier with an upslope would slowly force the cloud-deck to ever higher altitudes, and I could not be sure of just how high that might be after a couple of hundred miles of flight. Besides there were several broken cloud layers above me, and these might begin to merge with the low deck, leaving me with no escape but to retreat and hope that the conditions behind had not deteriorated. If serious icing were to occur, the situation would be hopeless. I would have no chance to descend to warmer air to melt the ice away because there is no warmer air over Greenland. The only recourse then would be to attempt to land on the icecap in what would probably be whiteout conditions, and which would probably entail the loss of the airplane.

By now I was climbing through 11,500 feet, surrounded by what really was a rich and beautiful cloudscape. A multitude of elongated broken layers were above. They exhibited some cumulus features, as though produced by convection. But they were each so thin and translucent that I could see the entire three-dimensional labyrinth in ever-changing perspective. Close by below, I crossed row after row of crests of clouds that are best described as stratocumulus. And drifting by were square sheets of stratus so thin that I often became aware of them only as they passed a few feet above or below the airplane. Off to the side, and seen nearly edge-on, these sheets formed a remarkable layered structure in continuous shifting motion. Once or twice I suddenly found myself enveloped by one of these sheets. Then I would climb for a second or two and be in the clear air again.

On reaching 12,500 feet, I leveled off at a comfortable distance from the dense cloud-deck below. Occasionally there appeared a long rift in the deck and I caught a brief glimpse of the ice-shield. I was then speculating as to the proper correction angle to my heading to compensate for my drift due to the south-wind, when I was surprised by radio chatter suddenly breaking the silence. It was the pilot of a Canadian aircraft (a Cessna 182), crossing the ice cap in the opposite direction, in the process of acknowledging a radar fix given by "Sob Story." My course across Greenland was within the so-called "Distant Early Warning East Military Identification

Zone" (or "DEMIZ"), which operates two radar stations, called "Sob Story" and "Sea Bass," constructed right on top of the glacier ice. Sob Story was some 80 miles to the south of my course, and Sea Bass was directly on my planned route somewhat farther west. Well, if the Canadian could get a fix, then I ought to be able to do the same. But I received no response from Sob Story to my radio call; probably I was flying too low for radio contact.

I then called the Canadian directly to inquire about the flight conditions farther on. He was on an instrument flight plan and had just requested an altitude change form 13,000 to 15,000 feet; he had been picking up some ice at 13,000 feet. I was told that I'd probably remain clear of the clouds at 13,500 or 14,000 feet— not too bad. But the surprise was that the southeasterly winds were blowing at 40 to 50 knots— much stronger than I had thought. Not wanting to overdo it, I held a correction angle of about 25 degrees to the south, and slowly climbed to 13,500 feet. We then agreed to call the other if either one of us substantially changed our altitude, so as to avoid the remote possibility of a chance meeting in mid-air in this otherwise desolate region. Some 15 minutes later I received a radio call; the Canadian pilot was relaying a message from Sob Story: The radar operator was recommending that I change my heading by ten degrees to the left for a direct course to Søndrestrøm; that wind must really be strong! And although I was unable to make direct radio contact, I was apparently being tracked by radar.

After about 45 minutes of flying between layers, the clouds began to break up and I emerged into a brilliant world. The sky was a peaceful, pure azure with an occasional isolated filament of white cloud drifting above, and blending softly with the blue. But the surface below was blazing; a brilliant white extended uninterrupted to the horizon; my recollection of the pack-ice on the Arctic Ocean was of a dull grayish white in comparison with the sun-reflector below.

I rejoiced in the clear weather; this is the way I had hoped to see the ice-cap; hundreds of miles of arctic land-ice, and nothing else. Flying is so wonderfully free and restful when enroute with unlimited visibility. When clouds are about and pressing in, I always feel a certain tension. And the release of that tension, when breaking out, enhances the feeling of freedom. Never mind that I would probably encounter clouds again farther on; for now they were out of sight.

I sat there, gazing out over the sun-illuminated expanse of white, so brilliant in comparison with the soft blue above. These moments were without time.

After a while I saw a string of what appeared to be dark gray patches, each geometrically in the shape of a V, imprinted on the surface below. They were the shadows of a narrow line of thin clouds. I soon passed over this line, followed by several more, and then saw the edge of a substantial fog bank, pastel maroon with diffuse edges, looming ahead. Behind the looming there also appeared a collection of crossing tendrils of cloud higher in the sky. The work of flying— which, as all work, is of time— was calling again. Because I did not know my precise position, I called Sea Bass for a radar fix; I felt that by this time I should be within VHF radio range of that station. Their curt, and professionally cold response was: "November-one-six-four-one-Hotel, stand by."

I was now approaching the maroon cloud bank, which, flying at 13,500 feet, I would easily clear. But the distant sky ahead showed a complex pattern of higher clouds. I remembered that the Canadian aircraft had gotten through all right, and I was hoping that I would be dealing with layers again— layers with clear air between. The thermometer showed - 1 4° C.

Quite suddenly, the fog bank below dispersed in a beautifully shaped cloud edge, and I saw again the brilliant ice-surface. But 20 miles farther on another fog bank obliterated the glacier. As I was approaching this, Sea Bass called.

"November-one-six-four-one-hotel, bearing: zero-zero-five degrees true, four-one nautical miles" was the no-nonsense delivery of information without so much as a single extraneous syllable. I read the numbers back, thanking the radar operator, but with some chagrin. Despite a heading correction of what I thought to be over 30 degrees to the south, I was 41 nautical miles to the north of my course; that must be a devil of a south wind.

I was then well beyond the halfway point in crossing the ice cap, some 70 miles north of the Arctic Circle, with Søndrestrømfjord about 120 nautical miles to the west, true. Although my route from that point on would be a few degrees south of west, my actual magnetic course was north-west because of the great magnetic variation which amounted to about 50 degrees. Add to this the large heading correction for the stiff breeze and the fact that the variation changed rapidly from point to point in this region, and navigation wasn't exactly a simple matter. Dense rolls of fog were below, and opaque layers above. Then, quite suddenly, I faced a wall of cloud directly ahead.

I looked over my shoulder to assure myself that the air behind was quite clear, which, indeed, it was. In fact, it was a wonderful and inviting sight. Beneath the edge of the higher layer I saw peaceful blue sky melding into soft, warm pastel shades near the clouds. It was a moment of complete uncertainty.

Of course I would enter the cloud wall ahead. But I was primed for an immediate 180 degree turn should I see any ice forming on the airframe. That much was certain. I was even mentally prepared to recross the ice-cap to Kulusuk, if necessary. The big question was the lateral extent of the clouds ahead. It would be very unpleasant to begin picking up substantial ice after a half hour of flying in the soup and not know which way to turn for the shortest route out.

All of this was clear without any thought. In fact there was no time for thinking, as I punched into the cloud wall, my eyes scanning the leading edges of the wings, the windshield and the thermometer, which registered -12° C. But no ice precipitated onto the airframe. And then to complete the anticlimax, I broke out of the wall of cloud after only about a minute's flight.

It was not quite time yet to relax, however, because I found myself in tight quarters between layers. But as time and distance flowed on, the cloud deck below dropped ever lower, and soon I saw the glacier surface. The cloud layers above were not quite horizontal, and on occasion I still found myself penetrating some wisps and streamers. But now the glacier held my attention; it was entirely new. It was of every shade of brown and gray. Its texture and patterns were most remarkable. It was heavily crevassed with an innumerable set of long, closely spaced furrows crossing my line of flight and extending without apparent end. It was obvious that I was approaching the edge of the ice cap, and I followed the shallow downslope in a gentle descent about 500 feet above the surface.

The long furrows began slowly to undulate as though following contour lines on a relief topography. In many places the wavelike pattern was striking; closely spaced and absolutely parallel, the lines were each of a different shade of brown-gray. It was clear to me that the waves were produced by the uneven flow of the glacier towards the edge of the ice-cap. The fields of waving lines were here and there interrupted by aquamarine pools of surface melt-water. A number of the pools slowly emptied their content in runnels of the same color, flowing down the gentle surface gradient. Although it was aquamarine, and indeed quite pure at the pools' centers, the color looked muddy near the rims. The runnels also showed muddy streaks. But in other places the ice banks were of a clean white, so that it seemed likely that the brown-gray coloring of the glacier was a surface phenomenon. Probably that color is due to atmospheric dust that fell in minute traces together with the snows of eons, which were then compacted to form the two-mile thick ice-sheet over Greenland. As the surface is now melting and sublimating near this western rim of the cap, the dust remains behind as a layer on top of the remaining ice. The white banks of the runnels suggest that the layer of colored matter is thin.

A little later the ice surface became very blocky, with deep and wide crevasses separating the unending rows of ice-blocks. The huge block-rows seemed to be leaning forward, downhill, with deep v-shaped cuts between, much like a rectangular chunk of American cheese being cut by a slicer with a number of parallel cutting wires. The surface as a whole was now also undulating with the first rocky ramparts appearing ahead. The rock did not protrude much above the ice. In fact, the ice appeared to be threatening to spill over the sawtooth ledge. But I knew that I had now crossed the glacier.

As I began to see more of the mountainous land ahead, I once again entered a world of color with many shades. It is curious that this mountain country was a good deal covered with tundra plants, almost up to the glacier edge. There were many patches of dark green, the shade dictated by the overcast which was then just beginning to break up. But there were also many steep slopes of barren gray-tan, looking down upon a complex pattern of narrow valleys. The sun's rays penetrated here and there in the distance, giving both warm and cold colors to the fluffy cloud edges.

I was then in radio contact with the Søndrestrøm airbase. Again, with no other traffic around, we launched into conversation about the beauties of, and life on Greenland. But there was also the need to relay landing information.

The Approach Plate, or instrument landing chart, for Søndrestrøm contains some ominous instructions. For one thing, the "Minimum Descent Altitude" for the instrument approach is remarkably high. There are, further, strict warnings against any turns to the north. And the amount of maneuvering allowed to the south was strictly limited. The single long runway was aligned east and west, and was evidently very near to a mountain wall on the north. The airfield was at the head of the 80-mile long and very narrow fjord, which cuts into Greenland from the southwest. The winds blowing down this fjord can be very strong, but are usually aligned with the runway because of the channeling effect of the fjord valley. On occasion, however, this channeling effect fails, when the wind over the ice field is strong, and at right angles to the valley, as on this day. And so it was: "wind, 190° at 19 knots," at precisely right angles to the runway. And there, among the instruments on the airplane panel, was the placard stating, "Demonstrated cross-wind component: 17 knots." Well, I would shortly demonstrate that the cross-wind component could also be 19 knots. I really had no other choice. It's true that I had more than enough fuel to continue the flight to Iqaluit on Baffin Island. But I had no desire at all to tackle the 300 mile crossing of icy Davis Strait, followed by another 300 miles, over land and water, to the head of Frobisher Bay. That trip I looked forward to, but on a fresh day.

I now recognized the local topography with the long fjord pointing in the direction of the sea, and was tracking the Søndrestrøm NDB. The airbase radar, whose antenna I could see on a mountain-top on the south side of the fjord, was also tracking and supplying fixes that indicated that I was very near to the airfield, no more than two miles to the north. But scan as I might, I could see no indication of a runway, or buildings one might expect to see on an airbase. There were clouds overhead, to be sure, but they were not obstacles to the view of the terrain. The controller was already issuing landing instructions. But these were all in relation to the runway, and required it to be in sight to be followed. I had quite made up my mind to fly directly to the radio beacon and then to execute the instrument approach, when I saw the west end of the runway sliding into view from beneath the mountain on my left. Now it was easy. After turning onto final approach, I "cranked in" a powerful cross-wind correction to the right, and, as if to prove that wonders never cease, made one of the smoothest landings of my flying career, tracking right down the centerline of the runway. Of course, the real wonder was that this wind, blowing over rugged terrain and dipping down a deep and narrow valley, was absolutely free of turbulence; it was "laminar flow," as is said in the trade.

The control tower and airforce complex are on the south side of the runway. In the narrow space between the runway and the mountain wall to the north is a low, but remarkably spacious hotel. "This is a hotel where you can never make a reservation," I was told by the operator of the airline "Greenland Air" in Reykjavik; they must accept all comers. Civilian operations are attached to the hotel, and here, among other compulsory fees, I paid $100 to the Airforce for an unauthorized landing.

A second low building, across a road at the back of the hotel, houses a small shop and the Danish weather office. After depositing my things in the hotel, I strolled across the road and up to the second floor briefing office. The weather briefer showed me the charts and said that it looked good for a flight to Iqaluit on the next day.

"That's too bad," was my response.

"Why too bad?"

"Because I was hoping for an excuse to stay on Greenland for at least a day."

"Well, if you want an excuse, the weather will be even better on the day after," he said, smiling.

I then went to have supper in the hotel cafeteria. The receptionist was a young Danish woman, but the cafeteria employees and the few guests in the nearly empty hotel were all Inuit, or Eskimo, as they are often still called in the south. The food was a delight to me. It consisted of thick slices of cold salmon and Greenland shrimps with some green vegetables and lettuce, some excellent hard bread and equally excellent beer and coffee, and a wonderful choice of pastries.

The following day I decided to make a short expedition into the surrounding countryside. I had noticed a trail angling up the mountain on the south side of the fjord, probably leading to the radar on top. This seemed to be a good starting point before setting out across the tundra. To reach that point I needed to cross the fast-flowing and silt-laden river, of a light metallic-gray color, which was carrying the glacial meltwaters down to the waters of the fjord. The mountain landscape was about half of bare rock and gravel, and half of patchy areas of low vegetation. But the rapidly eroding valley-bottom of the stream was all gravel and sand, perhaps a mile wide.

On coming to an overlook point, I saw two muskoxen in the distance below on the other bank of the stream. Looking up to the east, I saw the massive horizontal ice-edge of the glacier dome in the distance, whence I had come. My walk took me around the east end of the runway, among some of the airbase buildings, and finally across a wooden bridge whose concrete foundation appeared to be on the verge of being swept away by the eroding eddies of the turbulent glacial melt. Climbing up the trail, I was surrounded by hardy-leafed tundra plants and stands of low bushes forming a continuous hedge. Its upper surface was densely covered with leaves supported by a dense tangle of bare stems whose purpose seemed to be simply to lift the thin, green tundra-veneer about three feet above the bare earth. The two muskoxen had left the gravel flats and were now grazing this tundra vegetation.

At the top of the mountain I found an undulating landscape richly covered with a mottled deep-green carpet. Round ponds of shallow water lay scattered here and there, ringed by plants with small white flowers. A single reindeer with antlers in velvet stood grazing, and showed little alarm as I passed a mere 50 feet away. I came upon small patches of solid rock, black, with pale yellow stripes. The surface of the rock was polished as smooth as a marble floor. I imagine that the polishing was the work of the glacier, whose massive edge now dominated the high horizon to the east, and which in the not too distant past, undoubtedly was grinding over the spot on which I was now standing. I thought it remarkable that there were so few insects, and none at all of the stinging variety. But the cool air flowing down from the ice-field was probably the explanation for that.

On my way back I saw that two more muskoxen had joined the ones I'd seen earlier. I suppose that these animals do tend to herd. But, except for times of communal defense, when they form a tight circle with the prime bulls facing the threat around the edges, they don't appear to favor close contact, as the four were quite spread out over the terrain. Their long, dark shaggy coats sweeping the tundra grasses, and their massive pale bony horns curving upwards at the tips, and joined in the center on top of their foreheads like two bone-plates, give them a primeval appearance, as though one were walking on a prehistoric earth and could expect to see a woolly mammoth or sabre-toothed tiger around the next bend.

In the weather office the next morning things looked well for a flight to Iqaluit, although there was some question about conditions beyond that point. Well, I'd worry about that when I got there. I filed a flight plan for a route across Davis Strait to Cape Dyer, which is the eastern-most point of Baffin Island and precisely on the Arctic Circle, there to turn southwest, true, along a direct line to the head of Frobisher Bay. The first 75 miles would be over Greenland fjord country to the radio beacon on the headland of Holsteinborg. Then, over 200 miles of open sea to the mountain coast of Baffin Land. The briefer told me that I could specify "flight following" on my flight plan. If I chose this, I would assume the responsibility of reporting to "Søndrestrøm Information" every 15 minutes before and after the hour, to give my flight status, until I reached Canadian airspace.

It was curious. I had flown thousands of miles across polar seas and across the North Atlantic Ocean, and now, when the open spaces of water that still remained were growing relatively short, the remaining undertaking seemed like a tempting of fate. I readily agreed to take on the responsibility of saying "operations normal" once every half hour. On every flight leg of this trip I had felt a certain tension before takeoff, going through checklists, mentally scanning all aspects of the departure, evaluating the weather and terrain data for large areas ahead, etc. But once established at cruising altitude, I always felt a total release from that tension. It was as though the airplane was flying itself, and I had only to monitor its systems. I felt like a child, in wonder of the magnificent scenery, the dewy freshness of the arctic air. And the simple navigational chores, far from being a nuisance, added a richness, a kind of rational logic to the enterprise at hand. A sense of tension returned only on those rare occasions when the air was completely obscured by mists, or when I was faced with an area or line of towering clouds ...

I took off to the west and climbed out of the valley to a comfortable altitude above the mountain country ahead. The blue surface of Søndrestrøm Fjord angled away to the southwest in a long channel, obscured here and there by a triangular mountain peak along its shores. Flying over mountain crests and peaks, I often saw the surface of a branching fjord far below. The clear blue water and steep light-gray flanks of the valleys were half obliterated by the tall domes and curling filaments of sparkling cumulus clouds. In the direction of the entrance to Søndrestrøm Fjord a more extensive, but low cloud bank cast smoky blue shadows on the intricate ridge patterns of the distant mountains beneath them near the horizon. The lower edges of the clouds took on this blue color.

As the Holsteinborg NDB fell behind, I crossed the shoreline out over the waters of Davis Strait. The air was misty, and I could see no sharp horizon as the sky-blue waters below and in the middle distance gradually turned into a misty, light purple-gray where the horizon should have been. Occasionally, small lumpy clouds, loosely packed in square arrays, slowly drifted by over the sea below. Larger or smaller swaths of pastel purplish fogs sometimes enshrouded areas of the blue waters. Above, the sun was drifting in the azure sky over the Labrador Sea to the south. And then I noticed a very thin, but brilliant horizontal white line cutting through the purple gray mist far to the north where the horizon should have been on Baffin Bay. A single angular white speck appeared on the surface, in the middle distance to my right front. Then another, smaller one, in another direction. Then several more, all drifting in and out of view behind thin swaths of purple mist. These were enormous icebergs, and their perspective, along with that of the aggregated drift ice in the far distance to the north gave a sense of vastness to this dewy sea-scape.

As I flew on, I noticed that pieces of ice were aggregating more and more densely below until it became a continuous field of white. An area of fog then obliterated the field, and when the far edge of the fog bank passed behind I saw that the ice field ended abruptly in a long, gentle curve. After an hour of such scenery I again became aware of another kind of pattern, with its own, more pinkish hue, slowly emerging from the atmosphere far ahead. Its clarity increased rapidly until a complex mountain landscape, with snowfields and fjords, angled away to the northwest. A moment later I also saw the mountain coastline to the south of the cape ahead. It extended off to the southwest and its flanks were brightly illuminated by the direct sun. Remarkably, the illumination made the southern flanks more difficult to see. The intervening mist scattered sunlight so effectively that it masked the luminous land, sea and sky of the background.

I called the military station at Cape Dyer on Baffin Island, informing them that I was about to enter Canadian airspace. In fact, I was merely crossing over from one military Air Defense Identification Zone to another. Cape Dyer is the easternmost of a long string of military runways associated with the DEW-line. There is only occasional traffic at these DEW-line fields, which typically consist of a single gravel runway about a mile in length.

As I approached Baffin Land, its coastline some 20 miles to the northwest was obliterated by a lavender fog bank that seemed to be leaning against the mountains that rise directly out of the sea. I crossed the coastline at the point of the cape and turned southwest. For an hour I flew over mountainous terrain, clearing its crests by about a thousand feet. My course was a little more westerly than the general trend of the coastline outside and to my left, and after a while I lost sight of the Labrador Sea because of intervening peaks and their imposing mantle of cloud. But as I crossed ridge after ridge, ever a new fjord came into view below. Sometimes the valley was obscured by a cloud, so that I caught only a glimpse of water farther inland near the head of the fjord. Low speckled fogs of purplish hues lay over these water-tongues in deep valleys, which reflected the blue of the sky from their surface between the vapor puffs. Ice-fields and their glacier-tongue extensions lay on the upper reaches of the desert mountains of this easternmost part of Baffin Land. The clouds became more billowing, and rose higher as time went on so that their tops were well above the airplane as I negotiated a somewhat weaving course between them. And then they vanished, quite abruptly; I was again at the edge of the sea.

Cumberland Sound is a misnomer that represents a bay on the Baffin Land coast, about 150 miles deep and 60 miles across with an extremely irregular shoreline of hills and fjords, and opening into the Labrador Sea on the southeast. About 70 miles to my right on a fjord on the northern shore of Cumberland Sound was the Inuit village of Pangnirtung. It was a tempting thought to fly to the airport there and then around the bay to avoid another stretch of overwater flight. But the clouds seemed to be building over the land, and perhaps it was best to try to reach Iqaluit as quickly as possible before the convection became too intense as the afternoon progressed.

I continued on, straight ahead, out over the water. The shoreline just behind was of steep cliffs, gray rock partially obscured by dense white clouds. And I could see the white wings of seabirds gliding and darting about far below. Looking over the water to my right front I saw long horizontal layers of dark clouds seemingly angling higher from the equally dark distances to the west. The faint coast that I was making for on the horizon on the other side of the bay appeared rocky and gray and much lower than the coast farther north. A complex collection of clouds of all shades of gray stood over the land beyond. These I would reach in less than a half hour. For the moment they did not appear to be higher than I thought I could easily overfly. But I knew how deceptive the height of clouds can appear from a distance.

While over the water the sky above was blue, but a mistiness lay over the Labrador Sea to my left, and this mist reduced the contrast on the cloud-scene ahead. Looming above this mist was a single white dome, shining brightly from far beyond the cloud edge. It was evident that a thunderstorm was building somewhat to the left of my course far ahead. The forecast for Iqaluit had been for scattered low clouds. I felt a little uncertain because the air temperature was below freezing and I wasn't sure that I'd be able to remain clear of the clouds ahead.

The desolate, rocky coast neared, and I eventually crossed it. The pattern of clouds was quite chaotic, but I could often see the barren land through deep rifts. By this time the thunderhead, still many miles away to my left-front at about the eleven o'clock position, was towering and had formed an anvil high in the sky. Lesser cumulus clouds were building before it and also on my right, and their tops were by this time far above my altitude. Among these randomly positioned bulbous structures there also appeared undulating streamers of stratus. The perspective of this scenery was continually shifting, and by its means I was able to judge the distance to the thunderstorm.

All of this time I'd cast glances at the VOR indicator gauge for the beacon signal from Iqaluit. But the needle indicator remained flagged. There is also a non-directional beacon at

Iqaluit, and the fact that I had not acquired its signal I attributed to its possible weakness. Because the clouds appeared to become ever more densely packed, I finally requested an IFR clearance with leave to deviate at will so as to remain clear of the clouds. I made this request only to satisfy a technical rule in Canada that forbids visual flight above an overcast. The request was instantly granted because there was no other traffic anywhere to the north of Iqaluit.

The absence of navigational signals was becoming more of a mystery to me. To be sure, many beacons radiate weakly, but I would have thought that an important ferry station such as Iqaluit would have a powerful navigational signal. For the moment I was flying IFR with no radio navigation whatsoever. When I finally informed them of this, Iqaluit calmly stated that the VOR was out of service. It amazed me a little that I could file a VFR flight plan after asking for all pertinent NOTAMs and later to air-file for IFR, and receive no mention of the absence of a primary navigational aid at my destination.

For the moment I was doing my best to remain in the pockets of clear air that were growing ever smaller. I turned quite sharply, and descended to try to avoid a long white bank directly in my path. But it was no longer possible to stay clear; the open spaces had become too narrow and wound too deviously for that. I picked what appeared to be the thinnest part of a cloud edge that would take me around a large pillow-dome just to the left, and resolutely entered the opaque air. Of course, the "thinnest part" turned out to be seemingly neverending and I remained in this gray shroud for several minutes before breaking into a clear space again. It was very reassuring that no detectable ice had precipitated anywhere on the airplane. From this point on I was in and out of clouds, and I made no further serious attempts to remain in the clear.

After a time the clouds became more ordered and formed deep vertical open canyons. Then the canyon walls parted and

I found myself looking out over a bleak gray plain with a low topography of long lines of hills and bluffs at nearly right angles to my course. The plain extended far into the distance where the silver-gray sheet of Frobisher Bay widened out to the southeast into the Labrador Sea. Oblong, small blankets of stratus hugged the hills far below; this is what scattered clouds look like— I'd almost forgotten. The overhanging anvil of the thunderstorm, now on my left, cast the landscape in shade. Farther on, near the head of Frobisher Bay, the sun managed to push back the shade, but its illumination did little to remove the bleakness from this land. A somewhat higher hill-ridge forms the southern shore of Frobisher Bay. This ridge continues on to the northwest beyond the head of the bay. A thick bank of low clouds hung over that line of hills, casting it in a dark grayness. A single ocean-vessel of the distinctive long shape of a steel hull, probably a freighter, lay at anchor offshore on the roads of Frobisher Bay. It gave the appearance of a dark sliver on the silver-gray sheet of water.

The runway at Iqaluit is long and of a hard surface. The most glaring structure on the airport is a large bright-yellow cube with rounded edges and corners, and sitting on round pilings driving into the permafrost earth. The cube contains several rows of porthole-shaped windows, and the word IQALUIT is spread across one face. There was something art deco-like in the aspect of this new terminal which also contains the administrative, briefing and weather services of Iqaluit. It seemed totally out of place on this desolate, windswept land. A large, older hangar of conventional design stood opposite. And the ships anchored in the bay beyond marked this place as a crossroads of strategic importance. This seemed curious to me because Iqaluit is so far removed from any center of commerce.

I had landed at Iqaluit for the purpose of clearing Canadian customs and to obtain an update on the somewhat questionable weather before me on my continuation to Kuujjuak (formerly Fort Chimo) at the head of Ungava Bay in the north of Quebec province. The route after Kuujjuak was far from settled in my mind. It would be a choice between two unpleasant alternatives. The safer of these was to fly due south and to make directly for the area of Montreal. The more direct alternative was a long flight southwest over sparse forest and tundra, and then open water, to Moosonee on the southwestern shore of James Bay. These routes were unpleasant because the area to be overflown has a reputation for bad weather, probably because it is downwind from Hudson Bay. To this, the meteorologist added the unwelcome information that the ceilings would be very low under massive clouds if I were to attempt to continue on at all, even to Kuujjuak.

My time was now running short. I had been underway for a month, less two days. I looked over the satellite images and prognostic charts again and again in the hope of finding a solution to my dilemma. But such a solution remained beyond reach. Squarely in the center of Hudson Bay the weather prognostic charts showed the heavy block letter L, the center of a deepening low pressure system. All of the area of northern Quebec and all of Hudson Bay were enclosed by a scalloped border indicating the boundary of Instrument Meteorological Conditions. To underscore this abomination was the long line of a stationary front across the southern tier of Canada. And all of this was expected to roll back and forth for at least five days, generating thunderstorms in the process.

I sat dejectedly in the chair, reflecting that I had not done such a good day's work because I had not even managed to reach Kuujjuak, when the weatherman Fred Aronson suggested the brilliant solution to my problem. After having ruminated for months, quite literally, on the unpleasant features of the home-stretch of this trip, I was slow to recognize, and even slower to accept his "heretical" solution. This solution was an entirely different route, which my set mind approached as it might have approached the suggestion that the earth is flat. His suggestion was quite simply to stop banging my head against the wall of unpleasantness to the east of Hudson Bay, and to outflank it by going around the north and west of the bay. Heresy! How could I possibly accept the notion of landing at Churchill once again? And then to simply retrace a thousand miles that I had already overflown? I regarded that suggestion with contempt. After all, it would keep me in the arctic a while longer, would allow me to overfly such fabled places as Cape Dorset and Coral Harbor with a bird's eye view of the shining drift-ice-fields on the pristine Foxe Basin. It would give me beautiful clear weather, with unlimited visibility, and a possible tailwind around that ugly low over Hudson Bay. It would solve my dilemma at a single stroke!

I still wonder why I was so slow to embrace this obvious solution, with so much potential beauty in its favor, and with no real alternative. The meteorologist even suggested that I fly to and spend that very night in Cape Dorset, an Inuit village of historical and cultural significance. But the evening was approaching and I remained in Iqaluit for the night. It was late in the evening in my room in the Navigator's Inn before the balance of my thinking tipped in favor of the western route.

The following morning I pumped an additional 20 gallons into my ferry tank for the seven hour flight to Churchill. I overflew the gray, hilly foot of Meta Incognita Peninsula to the island-lined coast of Foxe Peninsula on Hudson Strait. Remarkably strong tidal currents created a standing wave as the blue waters rushed between the islands, trailing long rows of foam. Cape Dorset passed beneath on a small island off a point of land before I reached the eighty-mile wide Foxe Channel, the last substantial stretch of open water.

Blue sea lay before me, and both to the left and to the right, on my passage over that channel. But the direct illumination of Foxe Basin to the north was especially captivating to the eye, and imparted a light blue shade to its surface. As the channel-crossing advanced, individual rectangular ice-floes appeared on my right, and in the distance they were innumerable, and peppered the sea with floating slivers and grains. Small, irregular areas of the light blue mirror expanse, between scattered pieces of ice, were of a deep blue, betraying a rippling surface in response to isolated puffs of wind. Far to the north over Foxe Basin stretched long horizontal tendrils of lilac-tinted clouds which reflected their form and color in the polished sea. After a while the thin silver-gray curve of the distant eastern cape of Southampton Island emerged like a floating raft in this blue world of water and sky. A compact field of drift ice appeared as a white line on the horizon. The edge of the ice-field curved southward ahead, and the ice was jammed against the northern shores of Southampton Island.

In my log I wrote about the channel crossing as follows: "August 16, 1988. Left Iqaluit at 1503Z, liftoff. Passed Cape Dorset at 1648Z heading west to Coral Harbor.

"(1709Z) Hudson Bay looks deep blue to the general southwest direction from its connection to Foxe Basin. It seems I can tell that I'm circumnavigating a Low over Hudson Bay by the purplish haze over the horizon to the southeast and long strips of stratus above and below [my altitude] in that direction. Southampton Island is visible ahead — very low. There was some unexpected clear air turbulance just after Cape Dorset, but the air is now as smooth as silk. The magnetic compass is working, but just barely, and it tends to swing slowly back and forth (1717Z).

"(1718Z) Beginning to pick up the Coral Harbor VOR — have been navigating with ADF so far.

"(1731Z) Approaching Southampton Island — many pieces of ice off the north shore of its eastern peninsula — looks like packice to the northwest.

"(1741Z) Ice pieces floating on perfectly still blue water in the near distance — ice fields farther out — lavender stratus in the distant sky down to the horizon (to the north). This lavender color is reflected in the still waters in the distance among the drift-ice.

"Passing Coral Harbor at 1810Z."

Coral Harbor lies near the southern shore of Southampton Island. From the air the shoreline near Coral Harbor appears to be a network of dikes enclosing polygonal lagoons, probably a creation of the permafrost. Both the "lagoons" and the dikes are of warm pastel hues, quite reminiscent of corals, although they could not be real coral in these freezing waters.

Large white clouds began to build over the land to the west and southwest of Coral Harbor, and I climbed to 9000 feet to clear them. The edge of the actively building cloud layer coincided with the shore, and to the south the blue surface of Hudson Bay shimmered with the solar reflection. A couple of thin brushstrokes of white hung high in the sky over the unending sea in that direction. For several hours I was on top of a white cloudscape that reflected the brilliant sunlight, in which I felt myself imbedded, back into space. I passed over Chesterfield Inlet, Rankin Inlet and finally Eskimo Point. The cloud layer then began to break up slowly, and I landed at Churchill with clear sky overhead. A month later now, all ice had vanished from the Churchill River and from Hudson Bay. This was probably the warmest time of the year in these regions.

The flight south to the U.S. border was marked with scattered clouds and large billows of light gray smoke. The smoke was rising from many points on the forest, like genies, inflating, and expanding, as they emerge from the small openings of magical lamps. These forest fires smoked in every direction. There were times when it seemed that all of Canada was burning.

The last three-hundred miles were flown in solid instrument conditions. The wispy atmosphere was composed of a continuum of layers with varying degrees of translucence. After all this flying in remote and ever new country, the power of the architectural beauty of this fairyland cloudscape to entrance the soul was as great as ever. Just to the north of Minneapolis the clouds gave way to a thick haze and I began to perspire in the intense, humid heat. I was back again in the land of sweltering and stormy summers. But this was the final gasp of the hot summer of 1988. The polar cold front that I had crossed during the last hour swept southward across the Midwest. And only hours after my arrival that summer's heat was broken, and the cool weather of early autumn settled onto the land.

Calving glacier at the head of Otto Fjord, Grantland. Bottom: View of Otto Fjord (foreground) with Axel Heiberg Land on the horizon, left, and Nansen Sound opening onto the Arctic Ocean on the horizon, right.

Torellbreen on Spitsbergen.

GEOPHYSICAL EPILOG

The experience of flight contains many feelings of wonder, freedom and even playfulness. For some, there is a deep appreciation for the earth below as we see sometimes chaotic, sometimes ordered patterns of outcroppings of rock. We speculate on the powerful, relentlessly dynamic forces within the earth that are capable of bending (folding) and cracking (faulting) extensive slabs of hard rock to continually change the face of the planet on all scales from local to global.

I include this geophysical epilog as a cushion to the abrupt ending of a month of flying, but also because the key elements of the theory outlined here fell into place in my mind during the arresting view of the interacting ice-floes of the pack-ice on the Arctic Ocean. On the one hand, there was the obvious behavior of the ice-crust of the ocean. Wind and ocean currents, that is, *convective flow,* drives the rigid ice-crust sufficiently vigorously to fractionate it, and to build pressure ridges and cause "underplating." On the other hand, I was reminded several times of the visible surface of the sun, called the *photosphere.* When viewed through a telescope with sufficiently dark filters to make the the light-intensity tolerable, the radiating photosphere reveals the tops of what appear to be closely packed thunderstorms, that is, the tops of convection cells called "granules." This was the key to the theoretical convection that I needed to drive the surface "crustal" plates of the Earth.

I have mentioned plate-tectonics several times in the narrative of my flight. First proposed by the German meteorologist Alfred Wegener during extensive field-work on Greenland [8], plate-tectonics is today recognized as geophysical fact. Like the movement of the arctic ice-floes, the rigid stone plates of the solid surface of the earth are driven about by convective forces. In the case of the rocky plates, the subterranean convection occurs as plastic flow of solid, crystalline stone. This stony outer portion of the earth, called the *mantle,* comprises the bulk of the volume, and nearly half of the earth's radius to a depth of 2900 km. It is carried, like slag in an iron-ore smelter, on top of the metallic core of the earth. Radioactive decay of unstable nuclei within the mantle material provides a continuous heat source which maintains a temperature gradient across the mantle as heat-radiation from the surface keeps the outer layer relatively cool.

Mantle material is a relatively good heat-insulator, thus making the conduction of heat to the surface relatively inefficient. This leads to a temperature buildup within the mantle that is sufficient to induce convection in what would appear to be a most unlikely material for such a process, namely solid rock. Despite its slow turnover rates (hundreds of millions of years for a complete turnover cycle — the convection-speeds are roughly equivalent to the rate of growth of fingernails), convection is the principal mode of heat transfer from the depths to the surface of the Earth.

Much research has been done on the convective processes of the mantle (e.g. [9-12] as examples of some recent papers), but I think it is fair to say that we are only in the dawn of understanding the actual patterns of convection occurring within the Earth. In closing this book, I therefore wish to offer a hypothesis for the actual convection patterns occurring within the rocky portions of the planet. I must warn, however, that this theory is new and likely to be controversial because it is in some conflict with contemporary thinking (c.f. [11-15]).

For purposes of the hypothesis, we can ignore the "classical" concept of crust and consider instead the "tectonic" concept of *lithosphere* as the outermost basic building-constituent of the model Earth. The "classical" division into crust and mantle was based on geochemical distinctions that play no role in the physical theory of tectonic movement. The lithosphere contains all of the crust and in addition contains a portion of the outer mantle to a depth of about 100 km. Although the lithospheric layer is amenable to plastic distortion, it can be considered as a separate and distinct rigid layer because it happens to be floating as a unit on a partially melted rocky layer of the mantle called the *asthenosphere*. This asthenosphere is relatively thin (extending from ~100 km to ~250 km depth, as determined by seismic velocities) and overlays the remainder of the mantle below, which, despite increasing temperature, is again solid due to the increasing hydrostatic pressure. This is confirmed by seismic studies.

The presence of the asthenosphere, however, allows the physical processes of the lithosphere and sub-asthenospheric mantle to follow their own distinct courses. In particular, the lithosphere is cracked like an eggshell, and plays out its dynamics by "grinding" its broken edges against each other. Here again there is analogy to the action of ice-floes on the Arctic Sea. These essentially two-dimensional dynamics on a spherical surface contrast with the three-dimensional convection-dynamics of the mantle below.

The two-dimensional kinematics (movements) of the lithosphere involve the relative motion of some twelve shell fragments (plates) of diverse sizes and shapes that cover the surface of the earth. At plate-edges where the relative motion is divergent, basaltic lava rises from the asthenosphere to harden into new lithosphere, much as upwelling water in opening leads between ice-floes freezes (at least in winter) to form additional floe-ice. At convergent plate-edges, one plate is forced beneath the other (subduction), forming oceanic trenches and adjacent to these, on the upper plate, either volcanic island-arcs such as Japan, the Philippines or the Aleutians, or high mountain ranges such as the Andes on a neighboring continent. When two continents are driven into collision, the result is always high mountain ranges and plateaux near the "suture-zone," such as the Himalaya Range and the Tibetan Plateau. Earthquakes occur prodigiously along plate-boundaries. And all of this relative plate motion is driven by the three-dimensional convection patterns of the solid mantle below. The fact that the plates move at all demands this conclusion.

The following proposed dynamics are suggested by the existence of some 15 vigorous "hotspots" over the globe which are hypothesized to mark central upwelling plumes, or cores of toroidally shaped convection cells within the lower mantle. Hotspots are centers of high volcanic activity seemingly randomly distributed over the surface with as yet no clear correlation to the size and distribution of the lithospheric plates. Hotspots occur in the middle of oceanic plates (e.g., Hawaii), on continental crust (e.g., Yellowstone), and at plate boundaries (e.g., Iceland). Their relative locations appear to remain unaffected by the plate-movements, and as such typically trail a line of extinct volcanoes, such as the Hawaiian Island chain and its extension of the submarine Emperor Sea Mounts, as the plate continues to move over the deep source of the hotspot.

Imagine then that the slag shell of the mantle is dynamically composed of some 15 (more or less) convection cells each of "toroidal" topology. Their geometric situation is like that of distorted innertubes or donuts (i.e. toroids) lying horizontally, and squeezed together so as to leave no open spaces between them, to form a single continuous spherical shell-layer. The donuts therefore no longer have circular outlines, but form irregular polygons. It's necessary for me to interject here that the vertical flow components of the mantle are probably more complex than those suggested by distorted, closely packed donuts, and that there is lateral mixing of material at depth. The theory demands only that horizontal, polygonal flow patterns emerge at the asthenosphere, a phenomenon often observed in simulations. Thus, mantle material rises as plumes at (or through) the centers of these polygons, and then spreads out radially in the horizontal directions at the level of the asthenosphere, only to descend like enclosing curtains around the outer portions of each polygon. Viewed from above, hot material arises at isolated locations (hotspots) and descends along a network pattern, in the form of an irregular honeycomb, which defines the interfaces among the collection of closely packed convection cells. Mathematically, the irregular honeycomb pattern is called a (spherical) Voronoi diagram, based on hotspot centers. This situation resembles the "granular" convection-cell layer in the photosphere of the sun. The sun, like the earth, is a self-gravitating sphere of matter with an "inexhaustible" internal heat source. From the point of view of convective heat-transfer from a deeper layer towards the surface, the mantle cells and the solar cells play similar roles.

The particular distribution pattern of the cells is, of course, given by the distribution patterns of the lower plumes which may be associated with hotspots. Like the cores of isolated thunderstorms these plumes carry heat upwards from their bases [13,15], and, like thunderstorms, they are distributed in a somewhat random fashion. The original distribution of convection cells must have arisen in response to the particular random irregularities in the heating process, much as the locations of the rising streams of bubbles in a pot of water on the threshold of boiling are seemingly arbitrarily distributed. But those patterns, and the convection cells themselves must be highly mutable, and the mantle pattern has probably shifted many times over geological time, just as the turbulent pattern of boiling water changes in a chaotic fashion.

Of particular interest to the hypothesis is the two-dimensional pattern of convective flow at the upper surface of the convection cell layer, namely at the interface of functional contact with the lithosphere. As a first approximation, each cell generates a radial pattern, directed outwardly from the hotspot plume location [13,15]. Beneath each lithospheric plate one therefore finds a two-dimensional vector-field such as shown in the accompanying figure. This vector-field is interpreted as a force-field acting on the overlying plates by frictional coupling.

The strength of the plates themselves usually maintains their physical integrity in the face of this "discordant" force vector-field tending to tear each plate apart near hotspots, and to compress it in its horizontal dimensions, particularly at convection cell boundaries. But the plate usually remains intact. The question thus arises of whether the two-dimensional vector-field acting throughout the lower surface of the plate can mathematically be converted, so as to yield a simple description of the plate motions in response to the convection.

A mathematical theorem due to Euler (e.g., [15,16,17]) states that the motion of a rigid slab constrained to a spherical surface can be fully described by a single vector. This vector is the "angular velocity" and is represented as an arrow pointing from the earth's center to a pole around which the movement takes place. The pole can be far removed from the plate itself, or it can be on the plate, in which case the plate spins in place with no lateral translation. The net angular velocity vector of a rigid plate is thus given by an integral of a function of the vector-field over the entire plate area. The moving plate has its own surface velocity-field of motion dictated by its rigid geometry, and this plate velocity-field will be as closely entrained mathematically as possible with the geometrically very different asthenospheric flow velocity-field.

With the lithosphere set in motion by the underlying convection, the plates must now accommodate each other with regard to the conflicting net movements among themselves. At locations where two neighboring plates are diverging, relative buoyancy will fill the opening space between them with magma from the asthenosphere. The new lithosphere being so formed, and therefore being relatively warm, less dense, and more buoyant, will be elevated into mid-ocean ridges. Where plates are being driven into collision, one oceanic plate will be bent downward by about 45 degrees and be subducted. As the lower, advancing edge is driven deeper into the mantle, it encounters increasing temperatures and pressures which induce phase transitions in its crystalline structure. In this way, it looses its lithospheric character and becomes reabsorbed into the bulk mantle at a depth of about 700 kilometers. When two continents come into collision, portions of the contacting edges may be systematically sliced off (thrust faulting) and stacked up to form high mountains such as the Himalayas, analogous to pressure ridges on sea-ice with the interior of the floe or plate remaining intact.

This view of the rocky portion of the earth may therefore be summarized as follows. A continuous source of heat (radioactive decay of the long-lived isotopes of Potassium

40, Thorium and Uranium, and their shorter-lived radioactive daughter nuclei) tends to raise the rock temperature. But at the surface of the earth this heat is effectively radiated away, thus cooling an outer layer to form a tough cool surface "crust" (lithosphere). A temperature gradient thus builds up throughout the thickness of the mantle. This gradient is ultimately high enough to induce the convection of the solid rock, heat conduction and radiation being then insufficient to maintain the gradient below the convection-threshold. The convection takes the form of some 15 toroidal cells (distorted so as to be "area-filling") with central plumes. These isolated plumes first cause the overlying tough lithosphere to dome upwards, then to form cracks, and where cracks from neighboring domes meet, longer fissures propagate across the lithosphere [14]. (The East African Rift must be mentioned here as the classic example of this in our present era.) The innate strength of the lithosphere thus having been breached, net forces due to the lower convection set the lithospheric fragments in motion which is known today as plate-tectonics.

This hypothesis provides a connection between plate-movement and volcanism at the plate boundaries on the one hand, and hotspot volcanism on the other. It therefore has a unifying character that ties together a number of seemingly disjoint observations. This theory [15] has been quantitatively analyzed, and reproduces the observed plate motions with remarkable faithfulness [17]. Surface observations (hotspot locations, and the outlines of the surface plates) are sufficient for the theoretical analysis, and suitably tailored seismic studies (seismic tomography) with sufficient resolution of deeper regions may, in principle, lead to further confirmation in the future.

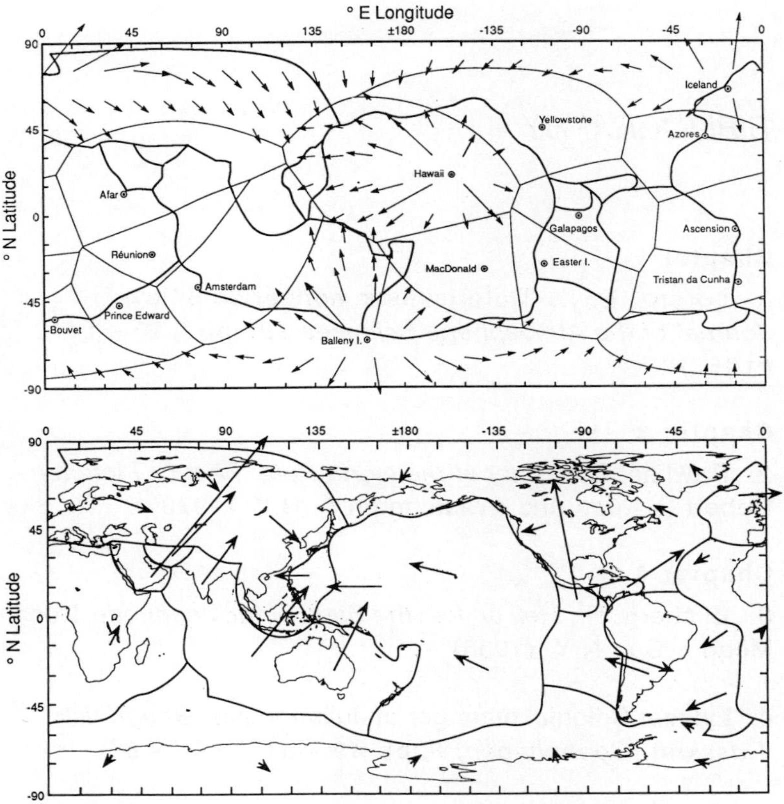

Top: Theoretical cells of mantle convection (light spherical Voronoi polygons) defined by a set of hotspots (identified by name). The convection velocity field (radiating arrows) is given for three convection cells. Heavy lines give the lithospheric plate boundaries.
Bottom: Direction, and relative velocities of the individual lithospheric plates as predicted by the theory (arrows).

BIBLIOGRAPHY

Chapter 1

1. Lorenz, E.N., "Deterministic nonperiodic flow," *Journal of the Atmospheric Sciences 20,* pp 130 - 141 (1963)

Chapter 3

2. Rawlins, D., *Peary at the North Pole: Fact or Fiction,* Robert B. Luce, Inc, Washington & N.Y. (1973)

Chapter 4

3. Ellsberg, E., *Hell on Ice: the Saga of the Jeannette,* Dodd, Mead & Co., N.Y. (1938)

4. Lytzen, Colonial manager of Julianehaab, *Geografisk Tidsskrift (Copenhagen) 8,* pp 49 - 51 (1885 - 86)

5. Nansen, F., *Farthest North,* Harper and Brothers Publishers, N.Y. (1897)

6. Payer, J., *Die österreichisch-ungarische Nordpol-Expedition in den Jahren 1872 - 1874,* Alfred Hölder, kaiserlich-königliche Hof-und Staatsdruckerei, Vienna (1876)

7. Orvig, S., ed., "Climates of the polar regions," Vol 14 of *World Survey of Climatology,* H.E. Landsberg, Editor in Chief, Elsevier Publishing Co., Amsterdam (1970)

Epilog

8. Wegener, A., *The Origin of Continents and Oceans,* translated from the fourth (1929) German edition by Baram, J., Dover, N.Y. (1966).

9. Gurnis, M. "Large-scale mantle convection and the aggregation and dispersal of supercontinents," *Nature (Lond.) 332,* pp 695 - 699 (1988)

10. Hauseman, G., "Geophysics; hotspots and mantle convection," *Nature (Lond.) 340,* p263 (1989)

11. Bercovici, D., Schubert, G. and G.A. Glatzmaier, "Three-dimensional spherical models of convection in the Earth's mantle," *Science 224,* pp 950 - 955 (1989)

12. Glatzmaier, G.A., Schubert, G. and D. Bercovici, "Chaotic, subduction-like downflows in a spherical model of convection in the Earth's mantle," *Nature (Lond.) 347,* pp 274 - 277 (1990)

13. Morgan, W.J. "Plate motions and deep mantle convection," *Geophysical Society of America, Memoir 132,* pp 7 - 22 (1972)

14. Wilson, J.T., "Currents in the mantle and the geology of continents," *Tectonophysics 187,* pp 61-67 (1991).

15. Fohlmeister, J.F., "Global plate tectonics driven by

mantle convection of a closest-point pattern based on hotspots" *EOS, Transactions, American Geophysical Union 71*, p 1630 (1990)

16. Minster, J.B., Jordan, T.H., Molnar, P. and E. Haines, "Numerical modelling of instantaneous plate tectonics," *Geophysical Journal of the Royal Astronomical Society 36*, pp 541 - 576 (1974)

17. Renka, R.J., Fohlmeister, J.F. and J.H. Stout, "Lithospheric plate motions predicted by a quantitative theory" *EOS, Transactions, American Geophysical Union 71*, p 1630 (1990)